Having It All

The 7 Gifts of Midlife

Ana Kandare Soljaga PhD

To my mum Bibi and my dad Bobo. For a lifetime of amazing memories.

CONTENTS

CHAPTER 1: YOU'VE GOT THIS
THE GREAT CRUCIBLE

Every day, people bring to me the pain in their heart, the anxiety on their mind, the weight upon their back. They discuss with me their fears and victories, their miseries and joys, their seemingly intractable blindness and wonderfully liberating insights.

And every single day I am in awe of their strength. Time and time again, I witness people who feel as if they are drowning in life slowly but surely start to swim. And then, as they and I work hand in hand together, they begin to swim with a little more ease, a little more confidence. Before long they start experimenting with the backstroke, or maybe giving the butterfly stroke a try.

And then comes the day when we realize that they are not just swimming anymore; they're swimming beautifully, comfortably, calmly. Masterfully.

Finally, the water is their friend.

Seeing such positive changes take place in a person's life is a thrill and privilege of which I never tire. Participating in the process by which a client comes to fully understand whatever it was within them that was blocking him or her from leading a healthy and happy life is a genuine honor. There may be work more rewarding than helping others to heal their damaged psychological and emotional lives, but for me there isn't.

If there's one thing I've learned from my decades of guiding others on their journey towards becoming the best versions of themselves they can be, it's that no one, but no one, is alone. By that I do not mean that no one is lonely. I mean that no matter how acutely alone a person might feel relative to the struggles and pains they are enduring, rarely if ever are they going through anything which is not, in some very key ways, common to us all.

We are all different, yes. But we are also all human, and so are all struggling with the same basic issues. We all want our parents to love and affirm us, for instance. We all want life partners whom we can love and trust with all of our heart. We all want to feel that the way we spend the bulk of our days is important and has meaning.

We all want to live a life that is joyous and fulfilling.

And because we all traveling on what amounts to the same road, we are all prone to falling into the same potholes in that road. Crushed hopes, failed dreams, loneliness, despair, the fear of being unloved or (worse yet) unlovable . . . these are the sorts of traps that it can feel as if life is forever laying out for us. And, indeed, we are often caught up in such traps. Because life, after all, is many things, but one of them is not easy.

None of us is immune from at least sometimes feeling as if life, in the opposite side of the boxing ring from us, is three times larger than we are, has twice our reach, and is in infinitely better shape than we could ever hope to be in.

And then *ding!* — the fight bell rings once more (with the sound, usually, of our morning alarm clock) and here's big, bad life coming straight at us once again, blood in its eye, clearly intending to leave us sprawled out on the canvas, so that it can dance triumphantly around us while we lie panting, aching, and dopily watching chirping little bluebirds flying circles around our heads.

Until, of course, we shake off that walloping, push ourselves back up onto our feet, and start preparing ourselves for one more round.

And that the people I work with every day *do* rise back onto their feet, and *do* stay in the ring, because they know the fight they are in is one that, despite whatever odds they're up against, they can win. I find it so inspiring.

It also often moves me to reflect upon the human condition—to wonder, for instance, what specific problems are, in fact, common to us all? With what exact challenges—what dreams, hopes, fears, and insecurities—must we all contend? And what kinds of coping strategies are most effective for meeting those challenges? What methodologies can anyone employ which will make it possible for them to stop living a life that hurts, and start living a life that feels good?

What *are* the biggest issues in life?

There are a few of them, of course. But what I have learned in my twenty-plus years of doing intense psychological work with others is that none of them is bigger than midlife.

Midlife is the pivotal point of one's natural lifespan. It's literally at the center of it all. It is the mountain range standing between everything that a person has ever been, and everything that they might yet become.

Midlife is *the* great crucible of life. It is that cauldron into which gets poured everything in one's life that has come before it—all of the raw materials, all of the elements, all the impurities—and out of which, if its transformational process is but carefully tended to, can come pure gold.

And it's this careful tending upon which everything depends.

In short, if you don't deal with midlife, midlife will deal with you.

Midlife is like a storm. You either see it coming, prepare for it, and then enjoy its wondrous power from inside a safe and happy place; or you pretend you didn't see it coming, and suffer the consequences.

And oh, what dire consequences those can be.

A MAN UNMOORED

The illusion that her marriage of twenty years was a happy one shattered for Jelica when she read the note left on the windshield of her car by someone from her husband's job.

Some two weeks later, Jelica and her husband David came to me for marriage counseling.

"Reading that note was like having the bottom of my life drop out from underneath me," said Jelica, while David looked down at his lap. "After reading it, I just sat motionless in my car, staring out the windshield, feeling like I'd been hit by some kind of bomb. It didn't even feel like a real thing that was really happening; I felt like a character in some movie I was watching." She paused for a moment, looking only at me, and never at her husband, seated in the chair right beside hers.

"But, honestly," she went on, "I think what felt so sickening about what I was reading was that I knew it was all true. It was like all this stuff about my life, and about the man whom I now know was only pretending to be my husband, suddenly made so much sense that, even as I was feeling shell-shocked, I felt stupid. Stupid for not seeing it for so long. Stupid for never putting the pieces together. Stupid for letting myself be taken for such a fool."

Suddenly Jelica turned toward David. She started off screaming, before quickly regaining control of herself. "How could you—how could you do this to me, David? How? How could you look me in the eye, day after day, night after night, and lie to me? Smile at me, and not mean it? Hug me, and not mean it? Ask me how my day was, when earlier that day you'd been sleeping with your secretary?"

She looked back at me. "Who does that?" she said. "What kind of person treats another person that way? Especially someone they've been married to for twenty years! Someone they've had and raised children with? Someone who has always been there for them, who has always cared for them, who has given them their whole life?"

Jelica broke down crying. "I just don't understand it," she said. "I don't understand how anyone could betray anyone the way you have me."

I looked at David. It wasn't hard to see how agonized he felt over the pain he was causing his wife.

"How?" sobbed Jelica. "How could you do it, David? Help me understand. What is it inside of you that lets you do to me what you've done?"

But David looked like a man who had been caught in a spotlight at the moment he was doing something terrible for reasons that even he couldn't understand.

"I ... I don't know," he stammered. He looked at me imploringly, as if hoping that I might know a whole special set of words he didn't, words that would help him explain the reason for the extramarital affair he'd carried on for six months before his wife found out about it.

Finally he looked back at Jelica. "I don't know how I did it. And I don't know why. I love you, bunny."

"Don't you dare," she said.

"But I *do* love you." Tears came into David's eyes. "I do. Of course I do. I think I just went crazy. I don't know why. I know men who've done the same incredibly stupid thing I did always say that the other woman didn't mean anything to him. But I'm begging you to believe that she *didn't* mean anything to me. She didn't! How could she, compared to you?"

Jelica cried, "Then why did you do it?"

David was again at a total loss for words. But I could see in his eyes that what he'd told his wife was true. He really didn't know why he'd done what he had.

And I also knew that for as long as that didn't change—for as long as he remained ignorant of the forces within him that were working against him—the bond David had destroyed between himself and Jelica would never be restored.

Contrary to the popular saying, what you don't know can, and most certainly will, hurt you, if what you don't know is why you're being compelled to act in ways that are manifestly harmful to yourself or others.

David needed to understand himself and his life better than he did. If he didn't take steps to understand and fix what was broken within him, not only was his marriage unlikely to survive, his chances for any enduring personal happiness, whatever happened in his life post-Jelica, would not be good.

The three of us decided, during one of our first sessions together, that while I would continue to counsel them as a couple, I would also start to see, separately and alone, David. It was wise of them to take me up on my offer to counsel David one-on-one, since their marriage could never really heal until David himself was healed. You can't ride a bicycle—or at least you can't for much of a distance—unless both wheels are in the same good shape.

I was not long into my counseling of David before I understood that a lot of his problems had been exacerbated, if not in some very real ways actually caused, by the fact that he was in midlife. He had reacted to the realities of midlife by having what we tend to think of as a "classic" midlife crisis.

But, of course, he himself was unaware that that was what was going on with him. He knew *something* was wrong, of course; nobody who spends their time betraying their marriage vows by living a secret second life doesn't know that something has gone at least a little wrong with their life. But David was so engrossed in the drama of the passion he felt for his secretary, the illicitness of the affair he was carrying on with her, and the nearly overwhelming tension born of maintaining the pretense that everything was normal when he had actually turned his whole life upside down, that he lacked anywhere near the perspective to understood that his infidelity was a symptom of his problem, not its cause.

As we all do from time to time, David needed help bringing the bigger picture of his life into focus. And as he and I, working together, began to achieve that focus for him, he was able to see that midlife, in and of itself, had caused him to become increasingly insecure about so much of his life upon which he had always relied for his sense of identity, direction, and purpose.

His father had passed away; so he was no longer the son he'd always been.

He was successful in his chosen profession; so he was no longer the struggling survivor he'd always been.

His children had gone off to college; so he was no longer the father he'd always been.

His body had grown flabby and stiff; so he was no longer the athlete he'd always been.

He'd been married to the same women for two decades; so he was no longer the passionate lover he'd always been.

So there David stood, a man whose identity, forged in the fires of life, had now been largely stripped from him by life itself. Which left him feeling lost, afraid, unmoored.

That is not a good place for anyone to be. Because people who feel that way feel desperate. And desperate people do desperate things. They hurt themselves. They hurt the ones they love. They make their lives worse because they don't know how to make their lives better.

David's story is all too typical of what happens to people who fail to appreciate and adjust to the fact that the first half of their life is over, and that the second half of their life can only be one of two things: worse than their first half, or better than they would have ever dared hope their life could become.

CHANGE IN PROGRESS

My good friend Mary is an enthusiastic and imminently knowledgeable gardener. Each autumn Mary collects into large bags all the fallen leaves she can get her hands on. Between her own yard, and the yards of her neighbors, most of whom are only too glad to give her the leaves they've raked together and bagged from their own trees, Mary ends up with seemingly countless bags of leaves stacked all over her property.

When she's collected all the leaves she's going to that year, Mary grinds them all up with her leaf muncher. She then piles the leaf mulch into the four or five bins she has in her yard, each of which she fashioned by simply nailing together into a box four wooden pallets. To those piles of leaves she mixes in food scraps and coffee grinds from her kitchen (and also from her neighborhood's restaurants and coffee houses, who are again happy to have the byproducts of their businesses being put to such good use).

Then, essentially, Mary walks away. Her job is done. She is now making compost.

Deep inside those piles of what most people could be forgiven for assuming is literally garbage, exciting things are happening. Microorganisms, along with worms and a whole host of moist little crawly things, are slowly but surely breaking down the rich organic material in each pile. By the following spring, Mary's leaves and food scraps will have transformed into the dark, crumbly, nutrient rich compost that year after year she relies upon to grow her perfectly delicious fruits and vegetables.

A compost pile is like middle-age. A whole lot of different and small things go into it—and then, under the surface, in a perfectly natural process, a whole lot of transformation takes place. What finally comes out of it is infinitely greater than everything that went into it. And all of it can be used as groundwork for extraordinary growth.

If you are in midlife, know this: you *are* undergoing a change. Things beneath your surface are undergoing a radical change. What you will be is not what you have been thus far.

Anyone looking to access and appreciate the magnitude of the changes that occur during midlife has only to recall the other period of their life in which they went through a similarly massive life transformation: their adolescence.

Remember your adolescence? Of course you do. Why am I so confident that you recall your adolescence just like it was yesterday? Because nobody ever forgets that most intense period of their life. Adolescence is, of course, that daunting, exciting, glittering-in-the-fog bridge over which we all must cross. It is, all at once, everything and nothing. The adolescent knows that he or she is definitely no longer a child, and yet is just as definitely not yet an adult.

Being a teenager is simply and wholly its own thing, a state unto itself. It is the ultimate period of transformation, reorientation, and radical alteration.

It is, in a word, powerful.

Adolescence is so enveloping and galvanizing because it's the first time in your life when you feel that anything is possible for you. It's when, for the first time, you're acutely aware of the full force of life coursing through your veins.

It's so intoxicating—and thrilling, and scary.

As teens these days are wont to put it, it's all about the feelings.

When you were a teenager, you had everything in the world going for you. You had strength, energy, vibrancy, and (if you were typical) you possessed extreme moral clarity. If nothing else, you knew right from wrong, and couldn't imagine how anyone could ever fail to distinguish between the two.

You knew your own mind.

You had it all!

You did, that is, except for one thing. And that one thing is absolutely essential for real peace of mind, real knowledge, real wholeness. You lacked what it wasn't possible for you to have for at least the next thirty years.

You lacked experience.

You simply hadn't been around. Or not nearly enough, anyway.

Your life, for all of its amazing potential, was still just leaves and kitchen scraps.

If you're in middle-age, you might have a lot of problems and concerns. But I guarantee you that one of those problems is not that you lack life experience.

And that you are now in possession of a full complement of incalculably valuable life experience is a crucially important fact about you which it is entirely too easy for you to dismiss, ignore, or take for granted.

If you are in middle-age, and you believe nothing else, believe that you are wise, whether at any given moment you happen to feel so or not. Because you *are* wise—or at the very least have at your fingertips all of the emotional knowledge that wisdom demands.

Because in one way or another, you've been through it all.

Now you really *do* know the difference between right and wrong—and, unlike your teen self, you know also how infinite the gradations of gray can be between the two.

If you've been living on this planet for, let us say, forty years, then you can be one hundred percent sure that you have now officially gathered enough knowledge and experience to live any sort of life you might want to live, and to become any sort of person you might want to be.

I am going to go out on a limb here, and guess that the sort of life you want to live is one that is maximally fulfilling, and that the kind of person you want to be is one who is happy.

You—right now, as you are, can have that life, and can be that person. You do not have to wonder whether or not that is for you a real and actual possibility. Of course it is. At this point in your life, it couldn't be any other way.

A WOMAN WHO KNOWS

Christine, a former client of mine, was married for nine years to Steven, a successful salesman. She was a senior administrative assistant for one of the top officials of the city in which they lived. The couple had two children, ages six and eight.

One night, at about one in the morning, Christine was awakened by a loud crash. Alarmed, she jumped out of bed. She found Steven on his hands and knees just outside their master bathroom, drooling and gasping for breath.

Her husband was having a massive heart attack. With shaking hands Christine dialed for help.

That morning's rising sun found Christine holding her head in her hands as she sat at her kitchen table. Her kids had slept through it all. They wouldn't be getting up for school for about thirty minutes yet. Steven had undergone an emergency bypass operation, which the kind-eyed surgeon had afterwards assured her went well.

He was now sleeping in his hospital bed. Christine had rushed home to see the kids off to school, gather a few things together, and then return to the hospital.

First on Christine's mind was, of course, Steven's health. Next was her children. How would she tell them what had happened to their father? How would they react to such terrible news?

And then there was her husband's business. As the top salesman at his company, Steven was essentially his own boss. And he had nearly one hundred accounts, businesses located within a two hundred or so mile radius of their home. Each of those accounts had to be visited and serviced on something near a weekly basis.

The doctor had assured Christine that Steven would not be able to work for quite some time. His proper recovery would depend upon his taking it as easy as possible for months to come.

Through the storm of worries whirling through Christine's mind was the reality that if Steven didn't service his accounts, the money coming in from those accounts would cease. And because of some financial business that she and Steven had only recently arranged, they simply could not afford for that to happen. This was an immediate and alarming problem for which Christine could imagine no solution.

But then she heard her children getting out of bed, and her mind turned to their care.

It wasn't very long after that frightful morning that Christine began to do the impossible. In short, she took over her husband's accounts. This woman, who had a job that was more than full-time, and two children who needed all the love and attention that children need—and then some, given the recent calamity in their lives—somehow found the time, gathered the resources, and collected the necessary information to step into her husband's shoes, to make sure that each and every one of his clients never missed a beat in their business.

First, late into the night, she read the file of every one of Steven's clients, familiarizing herself with who they were, where they were located, and what they most typically ordered from her husband.

Next, one by one, she phoned those clients. She told them all what had happened—and was, over and over again, touched to tears by how kindly they reacted to her sad news.

Would they be willing, she asked them, to, instead of her visiting them in person, chat with them about their needs over Skype or FaceTime? Every person she spoke to said they would be more than happy to do that. Most asked if there was anything else they could do to help.

A month or so later, as he watched her from the bed at home on which he was recuperating, Steven smiled at his wife. "At first I was worried about another salesman taking over my job," he said. "Now I'm worried about *you* taking over my job. I swear, Chris, my clients like you more than they do me. And they *love* me."

"They really do," said Christine.

"But they're ordering more from you than they ever did from me. Hmm. You know, I just thought, maybe you *should* take over my accounts. I could get used to lying around in bed all day, munching on celery and watching television. And look at you! Clearly, you're strong enough and capable enough to handle two full-time jobs, *and* all the demands of motherhood."

Christine laughed. "Barely."

"Barely or not," said Steven, "you have handled all three of those responsibilities, and more. And for the rest of our lives together, I will always think of you as the woman who, in a moment's notice, can become, if she must, absolutely superhuman."

YOUR TURN

What Christine went through, and how she responded to the situation that befell her, can serve as an apt metaphor for what any person in midlife is facing, and how they can respond to that challenge.

Christine was not prepared for the dramatic change that up-ended her life. (Luckily, midlife does not usually surprise us the way Steven's calamity surprised both her and him!) She had no choice in what happened; and when it did happen, there was no way to undo it, soften it, make it less. And it happened to the whole of her life, too, not just to any single part of it. It was like a tidal wave had come crashing down upon her house. Everything got turned upside down. Everything got soaked. Everything that she loved most in the world looked like it might get pulled out to sea.

And yet, she survived. More than survive, Christine thrived.

She assessed the situation, saw what needed doing, realized she had no choice but to do it, figured out how to do it, and did it.

Above all else, what Christine did was to call upon and essentially repurpose a whole lot of knowledge, and a whole lot of experience, that she already had in her back pocket when the wrecking ball hit.

She already knew the power of researching, organizing and prioritizing key information.

She already knew how to talk to people, how to tell them what they needed to hear, and how to be sure they heard what she needed to say.

She already knew how to employ (and teach others how to employ) modern communication technologies.

She already knew that there are in the world very few nuts that a lot of hard work won't crack.

Her husband's heart attack, combined with her taking over his business, was most certainly the first bronco of that size and ferocity onto which she'd ever been strapped. But this wasn't Christine's first rodeo.

So, yes, if you're newly within it, being middle-aged may feel very daunting indeed. It may feel painful. It may feel like a coffin you're lying in while someone slowly hammers nails into its lid.

It may feel like something you just can't handle.

But that, I promise, is nothing but you repeating to yourself an untruth that someone once told you about what you are and aren't capable of handling.

Of course you can handle midlife.

You've handled—even if it feels like all you've ever really done is be dragged through it—all of your life up to this point, haven't you?

You've made it this far, haven't you?

And that means you're still in the ring.

And that—right there, in and of itself—means that you have already won.

It means that, without question, you *are,* manifestly, a sur-vivor.

Believe me when I tell you that, from here on out, no matter how wonderful or tortured it's been until now, your life will only get better.

It should, anyway.

I'll go even further, and say that it's supposed to.

That it's *meant* to get better.

And to make sure that it does get better—that you get the life you've earned, that your middle age really does become the full delivery on the promise of your adolescence—let's now turn our attention to the seven awesome gifts that middle age is patiently waiting to bestow upon anyone who enters into its great hallway and simply claims them as their own.

CHAPTER 2: FORGIVING OTHERS (IT'S NOT WHAT YOU THINK)

THE HALLWAY

I really do picture midlife as a grand hallway, with a plush red carpet running down its middle, a high ceiling, mirrors along its walls, and soft sunlight shining at either end of it. In this hallway are seven gleaming, waist-high, intricately carved wooden tables. Atop each table sits a gift-wrapped box. Tied to the ribbon on the top of each box is a gift tag.

I invite you now to walk up to one of the boxes.

Having done so, you look at its gift tag. You see that it reads, *Forgiving others (it's not what you think).*

You lift the box's lid, and peer inside. What you find at the bottom of the box is a pair of ancient-looking iron shackles. The cuffs have been snapped open, and the rusted metal chain between the cuffs is broken.

FOUR THINGS FORGIVENESS ISN'T

Forgiving those who have hurt us the most is important. Because the degree to which we don't forgive someone the wrong they've done to us is the degree to which we carry around within us the anger, resentment, and depression that wrong naturally engenders within us.

If we let them, those who hurt us the most beat us twice: once with their original transgression against us, and then again by the emotional and psychological burden that transgression essentially forces us to live with.

In order for to let go of, or reduce to manageable, the anger, resentment, and depression that we feel for those who've hurt us the most, we must endeavor to forgive them.

That said, let's be very clear about four things which forgiveness is *not:*

1. **Forgiveness is not necessary for healing.** We often hear—especially via social media memes, and self-appointed "togetherness" gurus and the like—that we must forgive in order to heal. Nothing could be further from the truth. The idea that any of us are under any sort of obligation, moral or otherwise, to forgive another person for the wrong they did to us is ignorant, at best.

You do not have to forgive anyone if you don't want to.

You *can* forgive someone who has hurt you, yes. But you certainly don't have to. It's perfectly okay for you to withhold your forgiveness from a person to whom you just can't bring yourself to extend it.

You are the one who got hurt. So you are the only person in the world with any right to say, or even have an option about, how you should or shouldn't feel about the person who hurt you. If you are ready to forgive that person, great. If you're not, also great. One is not inherently better—not more just, not more spiritually enlightened—than the other. The one that's best—the one that's right, the one that's *actually* moral, because it serves to protect you—is the one that works for you.

As the song goes, it ain't nobody's business but yours.

Never forget that anyone who pressures you to feel, or to interact with another, in a manner that they are prescribing for you, but which doesn't feel right for you, is working from an agenda that's got nothing to do with you, and everything to do with them. But it's not your responsibility to use your trauma as a means to anyone's else's end.

You can safely ignore any person—and I mean *any* person: parent, teacher, friend, pastor, anyone and everyone—who tells you how you should feel or act to or about any person in your life who has harmed you in any way.

Let them go apologize to the people in their life who have harmed them, and leave you to find your own way to your own peace.

Another thing that no person should ever say to you, or in any way even slightly imply, is that your healing from the harm a person has done you depends upon your forgiving that person.

That is not true, at all, in any way, ever.

Forgiving and healing *can* go hand-in-hand, yes. But saying that you must forgive if you want to heal is like saying you must drive in a car if you want to visit a restaurant down the street. You can travel to the restaurant in a car, certainly. But there are lots and lots of other ways to arrive at the same place: walking, running, skipping, riding a bicycle, taking a bus, etc. And once there the meal will be just as delicious, no matter how you got there.

2. Forgiveness doesn't have to be given just because it's been asked for. People very often feel that it is their moral obligation —their emotional duty, if you will—to offer their forgiveness to a person who once hurt them and is now asking for that forgiveness.

One of the things which I think it's important for anyone who is seeking to heal from deep hurt or pain once inflicted upon them, is that they learn to simply *be* with that pain. When we are carrying around inside of us pain, and anger at the cause of that pain —and especially if we've been carrying around those two sides of the same coin for so long that now we're barely aware of what a burden it actually is—we tend to never at all consciously think about that pain and anger; or, if we do, we do so fleetingly, treating it as if it were some fly we need to bat away as soon as we hear its buzzing in our ear.

Not just physically, but psychologically, we flee from our pain. And that's understandable, of course. But it's not terribly helpful. By the time a person's emotional pain (or the dysfunction in their life which that pain is engendering) has grown so pronounced that they've come to me about it, I know that part of what will become the whole of his or her healing is that they learn, however incrementally, to be comfortable simply being with their pain.

You can't know what something is until you spend time with it. And the more complex that thing is, the more time you must spend with it in order to understand it. I don't want my clients swatting away the fly that is their pain. I want them, when they become aware of that buzzing, to be still, so that that the fly stops, and lands close enough to them that they are able to study the creature.

One of the benefits of learning to essentially be patient with our pain is that it teaches us not to react to, or from, that pain, until we've had a moment—or two, or three, or however many moments it takes—to know what's best for us in any given moment or situation relative to that pain.

Let us say, for example, that a parent who abused you throughout your childhood comes to you now, begging for you to forgive them. If you are not used to being with your pain—if you're not as intimately familiar with its warp and woof, its coming and going, the sounds of its very particular buzzing—then you are as apt as not to rather automatically offer that parent your forgiveness.

When, in fact, you may not be ready to do that. When doing that only makes things worse for you.

The fact that a person asks you to forgive them in absolutely no way obliges you to offer them anything but the sight of you walking away from them. Forgiving is not a *moral* obligation, in other words.

If a person who hurt you comes to you apologizing because of how bad what they've done to you has made them feel, then their apology is all about *them,* not you. It's not your job to make them feel better about what they did. It's their job to allow you to respond to the wrongness of whatever they did—and to their apology for that wrong—in whatever way works best for you.

It is good and even necessary to apologize to a person whom you have hurt (which is something we'll talk about in the next chapter). It's necessary for *you* to do that. But that doesn't mean it's necessary for the person to whom you're apologizing to respond to your apology in any particular way at all.

The fact of the matter is that if go into an apology with the hope or expectation that the person to whom you're apologizing will absolve you of your guilt, then you need to stay home and think a bit more about the role you played—and the role you now need to play—in your relationship with that person. You're not ready to apologize to them. You're still thinking about you—about your pain, about your need, about your desire to feel good about yourself again.

What you're feeling isn't remorse. What you're feeling is selfishness.

Bottom line: if someone comes to you wracked with guilt over the wrong they did you, then bully for them. You can choose to make that your problem—you can choose to forgive them—but you're under no more of a moral obligation to forgive them than you are to personally fix a broken street light that came crashing down upon your car.

You get to forgive whomever you want, however you want, whenever you want, and only if you want. Period.

3. Forgiving someone doesn't mean having to let them back into your life. I once had a client, whom I'll call Mia, whose brother, "Leo," eight years older than she, had serially abused her, beginning when she was four years old and continuing until she was thirteen—until, that is (as is, alas, typical) she was old enough to fight back, or to at least tell someone of the nightmarish things that he had been doing to her for all of those years.

When Mia was thirty years old, Leo wrote her a letter, asking her to forgive him for how he'd treated her throughout her childhood. It was actually more of a directive than a request; among other things, he told her that her being Christian left her no choice but to forgive him. (In the letter, which Mia shared with me, Leo did not once actually apologize for anything. If ever I hear of a contest for Most Passive-Aggressive Letter Ever, I will encourage Mia to submit that one from her brother.) Mia had received Leo's letter only days before she began seeing me, and was deeply conflicted about how she should respond to it.

"My whole extended family—including my brother—live in or around the same small town we all grew up in," she told me. "So I wasn't particularly surprised when the pastor of the little church we all belong to pulled me into his office and lectured me about how wrong it was for me not to have yet forgiven my brother for his 'misbehavior' towards me when we were children. He said he was terribly disappointed in me, that he thought I was a better Christian than that.

"And as much pressure as that was, it was nothing compared to the pressure my mother has been putting on me to forgive Leo, and to let him back into my life. I guess I'm just supposed to suddenly start pretending that what he did to me—what I know she and my dad *must* have known he was doing to me, since it went on for nine years, right under the roof of our very small house—never really happened at all. Like it's just something I should have gotten over already.

"That's actually what my mom said to me, that I should just 'get over it.' And my aunt is now constantly telling me the same thing: that's what's in the past should stay in the past, and that, for the good of the whole family, I should forgive Leo. 'All he wants is to be your brother again,' she told me. 'How can you deny him that?' Even though I've told her, on multiple occasions, what he used to do to me, all she can say to me is how much it's breaking my mother's heart that I'm keeping the family as torn as I am.

"And the thing is," Mia continued, "I *do* feel like I should forgive Leo. I *do* feel like that's the Christian thing to do, that forgiving my brother *is* what I would do if I were a good enough person to do that. A big part of me agrees with all of that.

"But the thing is, I have a daughter, a beautiful ten-year-old girl whom I love more than I thought it was possible for me to ever love anyone. And I'm a single mother." It took a few moments before Mia could continue, and when she did her voice was constricted, tight, like she was holding back her tears. And then she looked me dead in the eye, and with a ferocity that I knew I, for one, would never want to go up against, she said, 'I'm that girl's only protection.'"

I was so grateful that Mia had come to me in time for her to hear and understand that no one is ever under any obligation—and I do mean *any* obligation: not morally, not ethically, not in any way whatsoever—to let anyone back into their life, let alone anyone who has ever harmed them.

Let alone anyone whom they have every last reason to believe would sexually molest their daughter.

The pressure that so many people are so happy to exert upon victims of abuse to forgive their abusers—no matter the form or severity of that abuse—constantly amazes and appalls me.

"Forgive and forget" makes a wonderful needlepoint sampler. And there is an important truth informing those words: once we have truly forgiven someone for something they did to us, we do "forget" their offense, simply because there's just no energy around it anymore: the active memory of it dies a swift and natural death.

But as a moral imperative, "forgive and forget" makes no more sense than "frown and chop wood" or "ride a unicycle and recite poetry." One doesn't necessarily follow, or cause, the other. I can forgive a person for something they did to me, yes. But that doesn't mean I have to forget what they did to me.

And it certainly doesn't mean that I have to facilitate them doing it to me again by letting them back into my life. Forgiving a mad dog for biting me is one thing. Inviting that dog into my house is another.

Always remember: Never open your door if you don't want to.

Now *those* words I'd stitch into a sampler.

4. Forgiveness is not a constant state. We tend to think that once we have forgiven someone their offense against us, we're done with that particular affair. And most of the time that is the case. If someone cuts me off in traffic, for instance, I may curse that person for a minute or two or six—but, if I only will myself to do it, I can readily enough forgive that person (by, for instance, reminding myself that I don't know what might have compelled that person to drive the way they were: perhaps they were crazed with grief, or rushing a child to the hospital, or trying desperately to get to a restroom, etc., etc.).

I can forgive that moment of bad driving, and in that instant also forget it ever happened.

But for the big offenses done against us—the ones that deeply and indelibly wounded us; the ones that play a considerable role in much of what we've done and felt in the past, and in who we are today; the ones that have engendered in us so much anger, resentment, and depression that we've finally come to the place where we know we *must* release all of that if we're ever going to evolve into the kind of happy, peaceful people that we know we're capable of being—for *those* kinds of injustices against us, one moment of forgiving—no matter how brilliantly liberating that moment might feel—is not apt to stick in any permanent or constant way.

We can forgive something terrible done to us. But having done so doesn't mean we've also *forgotten* what was done to us. Some things we can no sooner forget than we can forget our own name.

And things that can't be forgotten tend to return to us in sudden and unexpected ways, for sudden and unexpected reasons. Life has a way of pushing buttons that we thought we'd long ago removed.

And when that happens—when a monster that we thought that we had once and for all thrown off our back by forgiving everything which created it has once again suddenly attached itself between our shoulder blades—the last thing we're often left thinking about is anything having to do with how erring is human, and forgiving divine.

Because at such moments we're not usually thinking about anything at all.

Usually all we're doing is feeling.

Feeling lost again.

Feeling hurt again.

Feeling sad again,

Feeling angry again.

Always remember that forgiveness is not an absolute state; it's not something that, once done, necessarily (if ever) *stays* done.

It's not just possible, but likely, that in the course of your healing process you will have to forgive the greatest offenses ever done against you, and forgive the person or people who committed those offenses. And, in one way or another, you'll have to do that over and over again.

One day you may feel so healed from whatever wrong was done to you that you experience washing over you a great and warm wave of compassion and empathy toward the person who did it. And then, the very next day, you may feel a whole other sort of wave washing over you—one that this time feels as if it is dragging you miles out into a cold dark sea, where it will leave you helpless to do little besides flounder, panic, sink.

If ever you feel that sort of forgiveness backwash, remind yourself that it is nothing to worry about, that it is all part of the process of healing, which very much tends to be a two-steps-up, one-step-back kind of dance.

Do not fall into the trap of believing that if on Monday you are filled with the joyful light that comes from your having fully forgiving the person who hurt you, then on Tuesday you cannot—or, worse, *should* not—feel any differently.

Do not, in other words, ever feel as if you failed the Test of Forgiveness. Because there is no such test. There is no standard of forgiveness that you have to meet in order for your forgiveness to be pure enough, or good enough, or anything enough. Your forgiveness is nothing more, and nothing less, than whatever it happens to be at any given moment of your life. When you are feeling strong, it will probably also feel strong. When you are feeling weak—when you're tired, when you're frazzled, when you're feeling like you've somehow lost track of the best of yourself— then your forgiveness might also feel weak.

And that's fine. You can handle that. Simply reminding yourself, whenever you might need that reminding, that forgiveness isn't a once-and-done sort of thing, is usually all it takes for you to stand up, and realize that the cold and dark water which you thought was once again threatening to drown you isn't even knee deep.

MARIE'S STORY

Up until she was ten years old, Marie thought she had a great life. She loved her mother, her father, and her younger brother, Henry, and they loved her.

And then one Saturday afternoon Marie's father disappeared. He swung his stuffed gym bag over his shoulder, told his wife and children that he was off he was off to play handball, and waved them goodbye. By the time Marie climbed into her bed that night, her father had not returned home.

When she awoke the next morning, Marie found her mother sitting at the kitchen table crying.

"She was wearing the same clothes she had been when I went to bed the night before," Marie told me. "I could tell she'd been up all night crying. There were balled-up tissues everywhere. It was shocking, and so frightening, to see her look the way she did. I'd never seen any adult look so devastated, so beaten, much less my mother, who had always been so happy and serene. When she looked up at me, and I saw her face, I couldn't even move. I knew something terrible had happened.

"She just stared at me for the longest time, saying nothing. I finally managed to ask her what was wrong. At first she didn't say anything; she just kept silently and so sadly looking at me. And then her eyes filled with tears. As the water ran down her cheeks, she said, 'Your father has left us. He's gone, Marie. He's not coming home.'"

When Marie told me her story, she was a middle-aged woman. But remembering that long ago morning with her mother, she, too, cried.

Marie had no idea why her father left. Her mother never really talked to her about it. As far as Marie knew, her mother didn't know anything more about it than she did. It was simply that one day Marie and Henry had a father, and the next day they didn't.

One day Marie's mother was a happily married woman (or so it certainly seemed to Marie), and the next she was a single woman with two children.

A single mother who suddenly had to earn a living—when up to that point she had "only" ever been a full-time mother and wife.

So Marie's life took a radical turn.

"My mother got a job with a domestic services agency cleaning other people's homes," Marie said. "They gave her as much work as she could take, and she took a lot. She wanted to keep us in our home. I don't know if my father ever gave her any money, but if he did it wasn't much. Eventually we had to move to a poorer neighborhood. The day we moved from the only house I'd ever known, my mother was so depressed—and so just worn out from her job, I think—that I remember being afraid that she might do something terrible to herself. I was petrified that she would. The whole time we were packing and loading all our stuff into our car, I never let her out of my sight. I was afraid to.

"My mother never really recovered from my father's leaving," she continued. "And right about the time we moved from our house into our shabby little flat is when she started drinking. I barely knew what alcohol was; all I knew was that bottles of wine became a regular thing in our house. Our mom was tired, unhappy, and didn't ever seem to have the time or energy to do much of anything when she was home except sleep.

"All the responsibilities that had always been hers now fell to me. I took care of Henry; I did all the grocery shopping; and I did all the cooking and cleaning. I did everything, basically. Because what choice did I have? Henry had to go to school. And he needed clothes and food to eat—just like I did. Just like my mom did. Somebody had to take care of things."

Three years after he left her life, Marie found out where her father lived. Between his leaving and that time, neither Marie nor her little brother had heard a single word from their father. Marie got the impression that her father had in some way kept or at least been in touch with her mother, but she was never sure about that either way. All she knew is that whenever she asked about it, her mother claimed no knowledge of his whereabouts, and clearly didn't want to talk about it. So, rather than cause her mother any pain about it, Marie stopped asking.

And then, when she was thirteen, Marie, through an aunt of hers, found out the address where her father was living. She knew that her mother was also in possession of this information. She did not tell her that now she knew it, too.

That Saturday, Marie told her mother that she was going to spend the day with friends. But instead she took a two-hour train ride to find her father.

And she did. She found him at his upper-middle class home, which had a well-kept front yard, and a white picket fence, and twinkling white lights all around its windows, because it was Christmas time.

"It was just the nicest house," said Marie. "Especially compared to the place we lived. It seemed impossible to me that my father could really live in that house. I just couldn't seem to make any sense of it. For I don't even know how long, I just stood there, right across the street from the place, staring at it. It was so clean, so neat. There was a Christmas tree in the big window facing the street. It was all decorated, and everything. I thought it looked like a house you'd see on some television show about a regular, happy family.

"All of a sudden the door of the house opened up, and two boys ran out. They looked maybe two years younger than Henry. Behind them came a woman—their mother, I assumed. And next out of the house was my father.

"I knew immediately it was him. I had wondered if I would even recognize him when I saw him, even though it had only been three years, and of course I would. It was so shocking to see him. It felt like I'd been hit by a bolt of cold lightening.

"The moment I knew it was him, I put my head down and started walking really quickly away. I didn't want him to see me.

"They all piled into the car in the driveway, and drove away. And that was it. I went home. I didn't know what else to do."

The next day, Marie told her mother another lie about where

she'd be that day, and travelled again to her father's house.

"I didn't have any sort of plan," she told me. "I didn't even know what I would say to him, or if I'd say anything to him at all. I just knew I had to go back. I think that, in a way, it was so humiliating for me to have to just duck my head, and walk away, like I was some kind of criminal worrying about getting caught casing the place, that I somehow needed to right that wrong.

"And I also just wanted to talk to him. I had missed him so much, for such a long time. Every single day for three years I had waited for him to contact me—to call me, write me, send me a note by carrier pigeon. Anything. And that message from him— telling me where he was, telling me why he left us, telling me that he loved me—never came. So when I saw him, I just . . . had to see him again. I had to talk to him. I had to know what had happened.

"The whole night before I went to his house again, I kept imagining him hugging me, and kissing me, and crying over how glad he was to see me. I really thought he would react that way. He'd been a good dad to me and Henry. How could he not be happy to see me again?

"When I reached his house the next day, I stood, just like I had the day before, right across the street, staring at this mystery home. Finally, something came over me, and I crossed the street. I opened up the fence gate of his yard, and started towards the front door. I felt like a zombie, or like I was on automatic pilot or something. My mind was a complete blank—except for this kind of roaring that had gone off in my head, like I'd gone deaf. I remember not being able to hear my footsteps on the walkway inside the gate."

"The next thing I know, I'm knocking on his front door. I felt like I was knocking on the door of a castle. I stood there on the porch for the longest time, and no one came. Then I saw that there was a door bell ringer, so I pressed that. When I heard the bell ringing from inside the house, it felt like my blood turned to ice. I couldn't have run that moment if I'd wanted to—which, actually, I did. But my legs had turned to marble columns.

"The door opened. It was one of the boys. He was staring at me expectantly. I heard myself stammering, 'Is the man of the home here, please?'

'Papa!' yelled the boy. He ducked back inside the house. And there I was—waiting to see my father. So numb you could have stuck me with a pin, and I wouldn't have felt it."

Here, Marie grew thoughtful, quieter. The pace at which she'd been telling me her story slowed down.

"When he came to the door, he looked at me like he didn't know who I was. He just stood there, staring at me, the same as I were a total stranger, just some girl who had wandered up to his house.

'Papa,' I said. 'It's me. Marie.'

"And then this scowl came on his face. All of a sudden he looked so angry. He pulled the door behind him shut, grabbed my upper arm, turned me around, and walked me briskly down the walkway and back outside the gate.

"On the sidewalk, he said to me, 'What are you doing here? You shouldn't be here. You don't belong here. Go away. Do you hear me? Leave!'"

In my office, remembering the moment, Marie looked at me with tears in her eyes. She softly shrugged a little. 'So, what could I do? I left."

Marie did not tell her mother what had happened that day. And she did not attempt to contact her father again—until, ten or so year later, she had a baby.

"I was happily married. My baby son was so beautiful. As angry and upset, as I still was at my father for what he'd done to us—for how he'd just *replaced* us with a whole other family—it didn't feel right simply not letting him know that I had made him a grandfather. Plus, I figured that if there was any chance of his accepting me back into his life, it would be because of my child. And deep down, I never stopped wanting him back. I never stopped wanting him to love me again. How could I ever stop wanting that? He had left a hole in my heart that only he could ever fill.

"Anyway, I knew where he was living at the time; he and his wife and two sons had moved into a better house, in an even better neighborhood, than the one I had seen before. It took me a long time to get up the nerve, but finally I dialed his phone number.

"He answered, which somehow caught me off-guard. And when it was time for me to say something back, I found I couldn't. It was like a clamp had grabbed my throat, like my whole jaw had simply locked up. But when the silence between us had gone on so long enough I was sure he would hang up on me, I said, 'It's me, Marie.'

"He responded with total silence. I was afraid he was going to hang up, so I started talking real fast. I said, 'I know you don't want to hear from me. I'm just calling to tell you that I'm married now, and I've had a baby. His name is Peter. He's—" And my father interrupted me. He said, 'Do you want money? Is that why you're calling, to ask me for money?'

"'No!' I said. "No! Of course not! I have a good job. My husband has a good job. I don't need money. I just thought that since I'd had a son, you might want to—"

'Do not call me again,' he said. 'Ever.' And he hung up.

"And that was the last time I ever spoke with my father."

"IT'S OKAY. I'M OKAY."

If anyone has ever had reason to go through life harboring a deep and abiding anger, it's Marie.

Do you know whom else I would bet has an extremely good reason to go through life harboring a deep and abiding anger?

You, that's who.

And why am I so confident of that?

Because you're human. And while there are not a great many truths that apply to every single human being who has ever walked on this planet, there are a few of them. And chief amongst those few is the rule that everybody, as deep down as pain can go, gets hurt.

And by the time you've reached middle-age? Well, by then you, along with everybody else anywhere near your age, has so often been so hurt by life—and most particularly by love—that whenever I walk down a city street, and see all of the people doing all of the busy and productive things they are, I cannot help but marvel that any of them is doing anything besides sitting in their cars, offices, or right there on the sidewalk, crying. Profusely.

Because life *hurts*. It just does. Not all of it, of course. Lots of life is wonderful fun.

But the parts of life that hurt are about as much fun as going to a dentist who thinks it's funny how regularly, severely, and unexpectedly he hiccups.

But look who I'm telling. If you're old enough to be reading this, you're old enough to know for yourself the pain and heartache that life brings.

And if you're middle-aged, then you likely also know—and if you don't know it directly, then I am sure that you sense its truth —how much anger you are carrying around inside of yourself, and how long you've been carrying it. And I'm confident you also have at least some idea of what that deeply seated anger and resentment is costing both you and the people you love.

I'd further wager that you'd love to relieve yourself of that anger, that you would much prefer not to live the second half of your life attended by that same poisonous resentment which you know has too much compromised the first half of your life. That you would like to break free from that particularly weighty and restrictive pair of shackles.

And that is something that you can do. More, it is your right to do so. No one has to live with anger and resentment that they don't want to live with.

By the time we reach middle-age, we have for so long been carrying around the anger we have towards those people in our lives whom we feel (or know beyond question) that it has, finally, taken its toll. It generally and most typically hasn't altogether destroyed our lives, but it sure hasn't made our lives any better.

When Marie came to me seeking counseling, it wasn't because her life was working so well. It was because she had finally come to feel helpless about fixing so much of what was wrong with her life. And she realized, as most people who seek psychological counseling have had reason to realize, that much, if not all, of the problems in her life were of her own making.

Chief amongst the problems she had was that time and time again over the years she had gotten into relationships with men who did not want, or even care about, what was best for her. They wanted what they wanted, and as long as Marie gave it to them—and asked for nothing for herself that they didn't want to give—they were happy. And that's the kind of happiness that, of course, never lasts long.

Marie kept getting hurt by the men she chose to be with. She'd been through two marriages, both to men she'd have been better never knowing at all. And her lack of discernment relative to the relationships she got involved in took a toll in her life beyond the strictly personal. It had also harmed her professional reputation. Twice she had been fired from the firm she was working at for having slept with a co-worker. In one of the cases the man with whom she'd had an affair was a subordinate of hers. And married.

And unhappy when she had ended their affair.

Marie had also developed an unhealthy relationship with alcohol, one that wasn't growing any healthier with each passing year.

Since you know Marie's story, you have at least some idea of the underlying issues which couldn't help but inform how she viewed herself, how she thought of others, the trust issues she had, and the types of decisions she too often made.

As Marie and I carefully and methodically unpeeled everything that was standing between her and the happiness she sought, we of course hit upon—and none too far into our proceedings—her father.

As you might anticipate, together we learned that Marie was angry at her father.

Which came as a bit of a surprise to Marie, actually. She had long assumed that she had put her resentment for her father to rest. What had happened instead, though, is that, as people naturally do, she had essentially buried that resentment so deep inside of herself (which she had to do in order to basically get on with her life—but more on that later) that it had been decades since she'd consciously considered, let alone in any prolonged way mediated upon or analyzed—that resentment.

But it was still there, actively burning away. She just didn't know it was still there.

She certainly didn't know how much of it was there.

But what the mind doesn't know the heart will make clear.

By the time Marie was middle-aged, the proof of the repression of her ancient anger was in the pudding of her life. And she was by then tired of eating that same, old, curdled, unhealthy pudding.

She needed a new recipe.

And the central ingredient she needed for that recipe was forgiveness. She needed to forgive her father for what he had done, and for the negative impact it had not just upon her life, but the lives of her mother and her brother.

But here's the thing I want to stress about the forgiveness that, if she wanted to free herself from the pain of his emotional legacy to her, Marie was going to have to extend to her father: That forgiveness, both essentially and practically, had *nothing* to do with her father.

Which I know seems counterintuitive; it's like saying, "You should take tango lessons—but only if you dance alone." How can forgiving a person have nothing whatsoever to actually do with that person?

Well, the first and most obvious answer is when that person hasn't asked for forgiveness. When we talk about someone forgiving the person who hurt them, we are very often talking about a situation where the person who has done the harm isn't *asking* for forgiveness. That's one of the big problems with this idea that a person harboring resentment against another should simply forgive the object of their resentment: What if the person they're angry with doesn't *want* their forgiveness? What if they're not asking for it?

Let us imagine that you have a next door neighbor who, one day, for no apparent reason, kills your dog—and clearly feels no remorse for having done so. If I say to you, "Don't you know that the anger you're feeling for your dog-murdering neighbor is hurting no one but yourself? Free yourself of your negative energy by forgiving the man!", the first thing you might be inclined to do is wonder if your neighbor is available for killing me.

Besides being all kinds of condescendingly shallow and inappropriately intrusive, the path you suggested I take is most immediately blocked by the fact that my neighbor hasn't asked me to forgive him. He doesn't *want* me to forgive him.

"Forgiving" someone who hasn't asked to be forgiven is like handing a bandage to a person who hadn't been hurt. What are they supposed to do with bandage? Tell you to go ahead and hang onto it, and that you'll be the first person they call the next time they cut their finger?

Here's the thing: All people who have ever been profoundly hurt by another person want the exact same thing from the person who hurt them. They want that person to take full and unequivocal responsibility for what they did, and to apologize for it, as profusely and completely as they can, for as long as it takes for us to feel like it is acceptable to us if they rise up off the ground and cease gnashing their hair and rending their clothes.

That's what we want. That's the dream.

They apologize.

Wouldn't it be great if every time someone treated you poorly they sincerely and wholly apologized for it?

Wouldn't it be great if cotton candy were good for you?

Sadly, though, in this world we have to deal with reality. And the reality is that most people would rather have root canal surgery done by a hiccupping dentist than to apologize.

And that fact about people leaves people like Marie, who really did need to relieve herself of the anger she felt towards her father by utterly and unreservedly forgiving him for abandoning her, her mother, and her brother—not to mention for starting a whole other family that he seemed to love in the way he could and should have loved his first one—with a difficult challenge.

And what do you do when you've a difficult challenge? You roll up your sleeves, tuck in your shirt, tighten your belt, and start working.

Moving from anger to forgiveness is like moving from one city to another—or, more, from one country to another. It's mostly just a lot of work.

But it's a lot more work than packing efficiently and making sure all your papers are in order. Mining from the depths of your heart and soul forgiveness of the sort we're discussing here is some of the most difficult work anyone can do.

What could be harder than putting yourself in the shoes of a person you'd rather grind beneath your heel? Than empathizing with someone who never showed you any empathy at all?

Than answering blows with a hug?

Than loving your enemy?

What all of this really means, what it all really boils down to —what we must have if forgiveness is what we're after—is understanding.

In order to forgive someone, you either must understand them, or you must know that you have done everything you can to try and understand them.

And the key to that latter part is that if you release just enough of the anger you have toward someone to allow yourself to intentionally try, even a little, to understand them—who they are, what they've been through, how they might have come to the place where they could have done to you whatever it was they did —then you will, in fact, understand them just a little bit better.

Which will make it a little easier for you to forgive them.

It's a formula as sure at 2 + 2 = 4. The more you understand a person, the more you can—the more you just naturally *will*—forgive that person.

We tend to think of the people who have morally transgressed against us as essentially heartless, cruel, lacking a moral compass. And sometimes maybe they really are such things; it's beyond the purview of this book to consider the nature, or proofs either way, of evil.

But it's certainly safe to say that most of the time the people who have done us wrong aren't evil.

They're just broken. They're sad. They're angry. They're afraid.

They're human.

Marie didn't have to feel a great affection for her father. (Though—and we'll talk about this later in the book—she did have to acknowledge and allow for the fact that the little girl inside her will always love and need her father—and that that's perfectly okay.) She didn't have to hear from him how sorry he was for what he did to her.

She didn't need to forgive him.

What she *did* need to do, if she wanted to once and for all be free of her anger towards him, is to understand her father—or even just to know that she had honestly tried her level best to understand him; that, in that very real way, she had given him every break, and ever benefit of the doubt, that she could.

She needed to think sympathetically and empathetically about him for as long as it took her to reach the point where she could feel how, if everything that had ever happened to him had happened to her, she might very well have done exactly what he did, if not worse.

None of us can change what another person did to us. But we can absolutely neutralize the anger that whatever they did instilled in us by digging deep enough into our understanding of human nature generally, and of our own natures in particular, to finally comprehend and appreciate how and why the person who hurt us might have been rendered so dysfunctional that they were essentially left with no choice but to behave toward us in the abysmal way they did.

The formula for the forgiveness that frees us from our anger isn't, "I forgive you." It's "I understand how you could have done what you did. It's okay. I'm okay."

As it turns out—and as she learned not long before she first visited me—when Marie's father was the same age Marie was when he abandoned her, his own mother had died a sudden and violent death.

Knowing this fact about her father's life was what opened the door that allowed in the sliver of light that grew into Marie understanding her father, and to her then, as rain falls from the clouds, forgiving him.

And in forgiving her father was she able to let him go.

Upon understanding and thus forgiving her father, Marie's shackles—the heavy ones, the ones bearing her father's name—were finally broken.

CHAPTER 3: FORGIVING YOURSELF

IT'S ALL GREEK TO US

The gift tag on the next box you approach reads *Forgiving yourself.*

Inside the box you find a pair of wings. You intuitively understand that, once you take them out of the box, they will expand, and fit you perfectly—that they are only waiting for you to don them, so that you will be able to fly above it all, just as light and free as a bird.

Except those wings can be difficult to get on just right, to properly adjust, to get working exactly as they should. Instead of gently lifting you off the ground and into a gradual and graceful ascent, they tend to pick you up for just a moment, before sending you careening downwards again, or to keep you suspended off the ground just high enough so that, your legs flailing about, you are helpless to stop yourself from lurching to, fro, and the other way, or from rising up and then bouncing back down again, like someone who weighs just a little too much for the zip line ride they're on.

If forgiving others is making a coin disappear, forgiving yourself is making one of the great pyramids disappear. It's just a much (ahem) trickier thing to do.

Chief amongst the reasons for which it tends to be much easier for us to forgive others than it is to forgive ourselves is that a person's offense against us is usually crystal clear: they hurt us in a specific manner, betrayed us by doing this or the other, broke an important promise they made to us, and so on.

Our clarity about what they did wrong to us allows us to properly measure our response to that wrong. In that sense, our forgiving others is a relatively simple (however challenging it might still be) transaction.

But when it comes to judging and understanding the wrongs that we have done to others—not to mention to ourselves? Well, then our view usually becomes a lot more muddled.

Why? Because if there's one thing that every person in the world is, it's extremely and radically subjective about themselves. Things like judgment and understanding demand the *opposite* of subjectivity. They demand *objectivity.* They require distance, perspective, context. Sound judgment about an intense situation requires sober detachment from that situation.

But when it comes to evaluating ourselves and our actions, most of us are anything but soberly detached. Most of us are more along the lines of drunkenly attached.

And when it comes to anything about ourselves, or anything we've done, that deep down we know, or feel, to be wrong, flawed, or morally suspect?

About *that* most of us are not only not objective, we're not even in objectivity's general hemisphere. We're on the moon somewhere. On the dark side. Hoping no one can see us.

Which doesn't work. It's too cold there. It's too isolated.

What most all of us want to be is, in a word, perfect. Beyond blame. Beyond approach.

Morally flawless.

Insofar as we all want to be perfect, we are all perfectionists. And of course we are! How could we *not* want to be the best possible selves we could conceivably be? And how could that be anything less than perfect?

The Greeks were really on to something when they conceived of their gods as being just like themselves, only so much better—

so infinitely stronger, wiser, talented, and powerful—that a mere mortal could only dream of one day proving to be so spectacularly amazing that they, like Hercules, are ultimately given their own seat on Mt. Olympus, the gleaming abode of the gods.

And as sure as one empire replaces another, countless Greeks did dream of just that glory, honor, and reward. They aspired to become—or to at least become *like*—the gods they worshipped.

Which to our modern ears sounds quaintly fanciful, doesn't it? — right up until you stop to think of how many people today yearn to be like what, in so many ways, are our Greek gods of today.

Think of our movie stars, our television stars, our singing stars, our sports stars, our fashion model stars, our social media stars.

Think of how many people yearn to be as great—as powerful, as winning, as charmed, as admired, as famous: as *loved*—as those stars are.

Greek citizens went to their temples to gaze up in wondrous awe at their gods, who looked above all like perfect versions of themselves.

We go to the movies, or watch a soccer match on television, for the same reason. As a culture, we, too, create and then venerate the highest possible versions of ourselves.

But, ultimately, we must ask—and right about when we reach middle-age are most usually compelled to ask—at what cost comes our drive to be—or to at least be *seen* as being—perfect?

We know that we would love to be perfect, and we know why: because being perfect would mean that we have, in a word, won. That we did it. That, unquestionably and absolutely, we made it. That we reached the pinnacle of what's possible not just for us, but for anyone.

That now, finally, we can't be hurt.

THE NOT SO MERRY-GO-ROUND

To be clear (and obvious), there's nothing wrong with wanting to be the best we can be. What goes wrong with that desire lies in how we define that word, "best." If by "best" we mean, "within reason," there's no problem. If by that word we mean, "the best *possible*," then a problem has definitely reared its beautiful head.

Why? Because we humans are an imaginative lot. Our powers of imagination—which come to us automatically—are matched only by our desires and our ambitions—which, like our imaginations, are as organically intrinsic to who we are as is our feet and our hair. Our imagination is simply hardwired into us. It's part of our DNA. Imagining is what humans *do*, the same as we eat or sleep.

So when most of us say or think that we want to be the best it's *possible* for us to be, we imagine ourselves—we cannot help but instantly imagine ourselves—as flawless. Beyond reproach. Wonderful in every way.

Perfect.

Which, of course, in real life—out in the objective world, rather than in the subjective world of our minds—we're not. Because we can't be. Because the whole idea of a perfect person doesn't even make sense.

Trying to apply the word "perfect" to humans is like trying to apply the word "greedy" to sofas. It's just not an applicable concept.

What would a perfect person even *be?* Would they, for instance (and please here do remind yourself that nobody ever said psychology was pretty) fart? Would the perfect person *ever,* under any circumstances, fail to be charming? Would they ever scream at their spouse? While asleep would they ever snore or drool? Would they ever get too drunk at a party, and say something that neither they nor anyone else in the world should ever, ever say?

Would the perfect person ever look in the mirror, and hate what they see?

You get the point: the idea that anyone could be perfect is manifestly absurd. It doesn't exist. It's purely imaginative.

But that doesn't make it any less compelling, does it? It doesn't make it any less *real*, basically.

Somewhere deep inside of us—and however vaguely we almost

certainly define it—most of us believe that we can be perfect. That we might one day be perfect.

And most certainly that we *should* be perfect.

And it's at the bottom of that slippery slope—the one that begins at "I'd like to be better than I am," and then quickly slides to, "I *can* be better than I am," before hitting, "I can be a lot better than I am," on its way to, "I can make myself so much better than I am I'd practically be perfect," before finally stopping at, "I *can* be perfect!"—that the real trouble begins.

Because once we have in our minds even the slightest idea that we can, much less that we should, be anyone other than exactly who we really and truly are—drooling, snoring, screaming and all—then we have already begun to sew the seeds of our profound discontent.

When driven by the desire to be perfect, we are bound to go nowhere at all. And that is if we're lucky. Most of us who are inclined towards constantly evaluating how we're measuring up to the impossible ideals we've set for ourselves end up either idling in place, or going backwards.

You know how it goes. You eat too much of the delicious chocolate cake that somehow ended up in your refrigerator. And that makes you feel rotten about yourself. The you whom you imagine yourself being—the you whom you think you really *want* to be—most definitely is not the kind of person who, instead of going outside to enjoy a beautiful Saturday afternoon, binge-watches six hours of Netflix and eats half a cake.

So what do you do in response to what you have (or haven't)? How do you respond to the despair that your own behavior has caused you?

But of course: you grab a fresh fork, and pull that cake back out of the fridge.

You cycle back in. You take one more ride on that not so merry-go-round.

You dig a hole for yourself, and then keep on digging.

The primary peril of perfectionism is not just that it sets a bar too high to reach. It's that it also becomes a bar with which even the most casual of perfectionists is bound to all too often beat themselves.

Voltaire famously wrote, "The perfect is the enemy of the good." Those are words to live by. And they're especially fine words to remember as we move our way into and through middle-age. Because by then we have lived enough, learned enough, and just simply tried hard enough to know that the only thing our desire to be perfect has ever done for us is hurt us.

In wanting only the perfect, we have ignored, maligned, or belittled the good.

When, all along, *good* is actually awesome.

Because it's enough.

And what's enough is perfect.

And that's something which, generally speaking, takes forty or fifty years to understand. And right about when you've got that many years under belt, you are finally ready to push offstage whatever notions you have left about who you should be, and to move on stage the reality of who you actually are.

Perhaps most importantly, you're ready to forgive yourself for not being, or becoming, someone whom you now know you never had any more real chance of becoming than you had of becoming the Wizard of Oz.

Before discussing the phenomenon of one forgiving oneself, let's take a quick moment to talk about the means by which most of us come to accept—however consciously or unconsciously—the idea that, come hell or high water, we are going to be—we *must* be—beyond reproach.

RECOGNIZING THE OVERLY CRITICAL PARENTAL VOICE

First, and to again be clear about this: Wanting to be the best version of yourself is entirely natural and healthy. We all want to continue to develop and grow, to learn and improve. You, I, and everyone else in the world was born to evolve. There's nothing wrong with that. It's what keeps the world going. It's great.

What's decidedly not great for us, however is when the people who raise us (most often being, of course, our parents) teach us, from the time we are babies, that we can only ever be as lovable as we prove ourselves to be. That rather than simply deserving it, we have to earn love. That the only valid measure of how good we ever are is how good the last thing that we did (or thought) was.

When our natural inner voice, which is always gently moving us toward a better life for ourselves by encouraging us to learn more, think more, and do more, gets all mixed up with our parents' voice, which (if we are unfortunate) is always criticizing and condemning us for our failings and shortcomings—so much so that we can't tell the two voices apart—then we, alas, are in for a difficult life.

Because we'll never feel good enough. Never feel smart enough. Never feel lovable enough.

And so, from the get-go, what a lot of us do with this "truth" we've inherited about ourselves is to fight like crazy against it. We do everything we can, all the time, to prove to our parents, to the world, and to ourselves that we *are* good enough to love.

And we're absolutely right about that. We most certainly are worthy of love.

Of course we are!

But not because of anything we do, or say, or have ever done or said.

We're worthy of love for the simple and glorious fact that we're alive. That we're human. That we're here. It's got nothing to do with good or bad, or better or worse, or deserving or undeserving. It's got nothing to do with anything except the intrinsic and inviolate value of simply being.

To be *is* to be lovable.

And it's *certainly* to be lovable to your parents.

And yet, somehow, as so many of us know all too well, the love of many parents turns out, in its application if not its intention, to be less a force of encouragement and empowerment than one of discouragement and hopelessness. Why exactly that so often happens is a subject for another book. For now, let us only make sure that we're perfectly clear on the fact that one of the hands-down best benefits of being middle-age is that you can finally tell the difference—or even just *begin* to tell the difference, which in itself is extremely exciting and liberating—between your intrinsically trustworthy inner voice telling you what's right and wrong, and your parents' overly critical voice (which you've internalized) telling you what's right and wrong about *you.*

It's during their middle-age years that people most typically begin to realize that that toxic, or at the very least that profoundly unhelpful, voice which they've been hearing inside of themselves their whole lives long—the voice that never stops judging and evaluating everything they do—isn't their voice at all.

Since they can remember it sure has always *sounded* like their voice, they know.

But then they realize that it never, ever was. That it was always the voice of one or both of their parents.

And once they learn to discern which voice is which, they learn to turn off the voice that's never done them a lick of good—the one that's always hurt them, that's always making a point of noting, yet again, how they failed to miss the mark.

And once they learn they have the power to turn that voice off, a whole new day for them begins.

THE REAL DEAL AND NOT SO MUCH

Before moving on to talk about the how's and why's of forgiving yourself by essentially surrendering perfectionism and embracing self-love, let's spend a few minutes talking about regret—about those feelings, or that knowledge, that we all carry around inside of ourselves that there really are things that we really have done or said for which we really do need forgiveness.

Let's talk, in other words, about our guilt.

We are all, in a very real way, veritable guilt machines. Within ourselves, and towards ourselves, we constantly and spontaneously create a whole lot of guilt—and thus a whole lot of guilt's offspring, regret. And guilt and regret are like sea air to an un-painted automobile: a caustic catalyst of deterioration which, if we ever really want to go anywhere, has to be scrubbed away.

But how exactly do we do that? How do we even begin to effect-ively assess or evaluate, let alone resolve, the giant, tangled wad of guilt that we're hauling around inside of ourselves—especially as much of it as we've tended to accrue by the time we've entered our fourth or five decade of life?

I would suggest that we begin by dividing our offenses—the things we've done for which we feel or know we do indeed need forgiving—into two separate categories. I call these two categor-ies The Real Deal and Not So Much.

In The Real Deal category of our offenses are those things that we have done and said which really do call for our redressing. In the category of Not So Much, I place all of those offenses which don't objectively qualify as offenses at all.

In other words, there are those guilt-generating offenses which leave someone to whom we do in fact need to apologize (The Real Deal), and those that don't (Not So Much).

If I feel guilty because at my job I took credit for someone else's work, that's a Real Deal offense: I need to apologize to the person I wronged, and take whatever steps are necessary to make that whole situation right. But if I feel guilty for not going to the gym often enough, that's a Not So Much offense, since it results in no one to whom I owe an apology.

There is the guilt born of bringing some real measure of harm to another, and the guilt born of failing to measure up to the stand-ard we have within ourselves for how wonderfully flawless we should always be.

There's failing another, and there's "failing" ourselves.

One of those is real, and matters. But the other one? Not so much.

If you seriously and deeply contemplate the matter, you will, I promise, find that a mere one percent of the guilt which is more or less always dogging you belongs in The Real Deal category. In the next section we'll talk about how to handle this small but critical fraction of your offenses.

The other ninety-nine percent of your "offenses" fall squarely within the Not So Much category.

The wonderful news is that all of your Not So Much offenses can be forgiven—by you, to you, and for you! — with no more trouble than it takes to blow the seeds off a dandelion.

Except that before you pucker up for that, there is one thing you must do first. And it's a thing that, for a lot of people, is well-nigh impossible. But do it you must, or (and here I will channel the great and powerful Yoda) forgive yourself you cannot.

What you must do before you can forgive yourself is admit that you're human.

That you're flawed. That you're not perfect. That you *can't* be perfect.

That you don't even want to be perfect.

And the main reason for which you should be able to easily do that is because you know that people who insist upon thinking of themselves, or appearing to others, as perfect, are not being honest with themselves. And that they're compelled to be dishonest with themselves in this regard is utterly understandable. We can feel for such people, because we know that ultimately they're only trying to please their parents, to prove themselves worthy of the love that should have come to them unearned. That's a fire that starts in childhood, and can burn one's whole life long.

We can feel for such a person, yes. Of course! But none of us has to *be* such a person.

You don't have to be slave to the praise you can never win anyway. You don't have to keep running the race that has no finish line. You don't have to keep fighting.

You can stop. You can relax.

Sure, you don't recycle every chance you get. Yes, you're sometimes less gracious to others than you could be. Of course, you could accomplish more in any given day than you do.

But guess what? So could literally everybody else who's ever walked this planet.

Like everyone else, you have a choice. You can either stay up on the stage, all alone in the spotlight—or you can yell for the spotlight to be turned off, peer out into the audience, see there's no one at all sitting there watching your show anyway, climb down off the stage, and step outside.

That's where everybody else is.

Why shouldn't you join the crowd?

MAKING AMENDS

Learning to say "I'm sorry" is something most of us learn in preschool. It's that core to human interactions.

Since no one is perfect, everyone must learn to apologize.

Children find it refreshingly easy to apologize. Why? Because they haven't been alive long enough to have invested a whole lot in any particular image of themselves which they then feel compelled to defend.

As adults, though, we have. For us an apology feels like an admittance that we're seriously and fundamentally flawed.

To be flawed is to be weak.

To be weak is to be vulnerable.

To be vulnerable is to be at the front of the line when the suffering begins.

Ergo, we are—we *must* be—perfect.

That's a chain of reasoning which for most people instantly strings together and becomes one whole powerful "truth." And what that most usually means is that if I (for instance) have done something mean or wrong to another person, I am probably going to choose to live with what that creates in me rather than apologize to the person I hurt. Because at least that shame of mine is contained, isolated, under control. At least it's not known to the world. At least no one *else* can use it to shame me. And if the cost of keeping that shame and regret bottled up inside of me is my own anger, or depression, or persistent feeling that I am not a person whom I can be proud to be, then that's just the cost of doing business.

At least I'm safe, right?

Right?

Of course that's not right. It's like saying, "Yes, while drunk I got angry and stomped a hole in the bottom of this canoe I'm in. But look at all those people on the shore! I don't want any of them to know that I drank too much and put a hole in the bottom of my boat. So I'm just going to sit right here in my canoe, and pretend like nothing at all's gone wrong. That'll work."

But no, that won't work. You'll just slowly but surely sink.

Think about the things you've done in your life for which you feel deep, genuine, and deserved regret. As I mentioned above, I would guess there won't be all that many such things.

But there will be a few of them.

So think about it. Spend some time making sure you get the big ones.

Write them down. Make a list of the people you've hurt bad enough so that you know you should apologize to them.

And then—guess what?—apologize to them! Call them up. Find them. Write them. Do whatever you have to do in order to make things right between you and them. And in so doing will you also make right everything between you and you.

If there is anyone on your list with whom you simply cannot make amends—people, for instance, who have passed on—then give yourself some solid alone time, sit down, close your eyes, and think of them. Call their spirits to your mind, your heart, your soul. Even if you don't believe in the afterlife, conjure before your mind's eye the totality of everything you ever knew them to be.

In short, if you can't connect with someone on this plane, connect with them on the next. At the very least imagine, with all your heart, that you have.

And when, in spirit, you feel that they are with you and listening, begin your apology to them.

Now, about that, and any apology you offer.

There are apologies—and then there are apologies. Make sure that every one of your apologies is a *real* apology. A true apology. An honest apology. A *humble* apology.

Take all pains to be sure that your apology:

1. Contains no agenda whatsoever for the person to whom you're apologizing. This needs to be all about the harm you did to them, and nothing at all about you or your needs. If you're going into your apology hoping that they will do or say anything in particular in response to that apology—such as forgive you—then don't apologize to them. Because you're not really ready to.

2. Contains no reference whatsoever to anything having *anything* to do with how they interacted with you, or how they behaved, or what they said or did, or didn't say or didn't do, back when the incident occurred for which you're now apologizing. The moment you feel yourself about to say anything at all along the lines of "Well, but you ..." or "Well, if you hadn't ..." stop. Don't say it. If you're not willing to take full and complete responsibility for what went wrong between you and the person to whom you're apologizing, then you're not ready to start that apology in the first place. So, again, don't.

3. Contains space for your attentively and deferentially listening to the other person. It can't be just you talking. It should be you talking—and then doing all the listening that the other person would like you to do. And you keep listening, for as long as it takes them to say everything they want to say to you.

4. Contains, if appropriate, actual (and generous) restitution on your part. An apology that's only words, when there are also things that could be done by way of showing or proving sincere contrition, isn't a real apology at all. And, just like everyone else, the person to whom you're apologizing is aware of that. So prove to them how sorry you are by offering to do for them anything you might which would make things better between the two of you. If you're going to talk the talk, then walk the walk.

5. Contains not a whit—not a sniff, not a hint, *no*—drama or histrionics on your part. Keep it real. And that means keeping it calm. Peaceful. Sincere. It means keeping it honest.

The great thing about apologizing is that, once done—and assuming it's been done as properly and thoroughly as it can possibly be—you *do* get forgiven for whatever offense you're apologizing for. Which isn't to say that the person to whom you apologize will always forgive you your transgression against them. Sometimes they will; sometimes they won't.

But knowing that you've done your absolute level best to make amends to someone whom you've hurt relieves you of a lot, if not all, of the guilt that you've been carrying around for that action. Once you've apologized for it, *you,* at least, can forgive you for the wrong you did.

By apologizing, you've done something honorable. You've done the only thing you can do: you've apologized; you've taken full responsibility for what you did; you've offered to do anything and everything you can to right what you did wrong.

The other person is, of course, free to respond to your apology in whatever way they do. You can hope that your apology results in their feeling that maybe, after all, you're not the person they might have always assumed you to be. After your apology to them, they may like you a little, or a lot, more than they had.

Either way, you are certain to like yourself more than you had. And that is a very, very long way from nothing.

LOVING YOURSELF

When we talk about how to forgive yourself, we're really talking about how to love yourself. It is easy, after all, to forgive someone you love—and especially to forgive them for the kind of small, everyday "offenses" for which so many of us tend to chastise ourselves so harshly, and, well, unforgivingly.

The short of it is this: We cannot forgive ourselves—or at least not in any sort of ongoing and consistent way—until we love ourselves.

Of course, "Love yourself!" is like "Climb Mt. Everest!" It's something much easier said than done.

But unlike climbing Mt. Everest, learning to love yourself is something you must do if you want to live a happy and rewarding life. Trying to live a happy and rewarding life when you don't love the person you are is like trying to climb Mt. Everest while wearing roller skates. You might now and then make a little progress, sure. But basically you're only going to get nowhere.

So what's the quickest, surest step you can take towards the goal of loving yourself? It's the step that takes you from who and where you are right now, to *accepting* who and where you are right now.

Forgiving yourself is *all* about accepting yourself.

And what, in particular, is challenging about that? What is it that is most likely standing between you and your acceptance of you?

But of course: It's your idea of who you *should* be. Of who you *could* be. Of who you *might* be, if only you tried a little harder, accomplished a little more, made yourself just a little more admirable.

Accept a loser like you? Ha! Never!

That's the core idea that most people carry around inside of themselves, as deeply buried within them as it might be.

It is in middle-age that this grip we so tightly keep on the idea that we should be better than we are—that we'll never be as happy as we could be until we make of ourselves the person we could be—starts to loosen. Why then? Because when it comes to the long and hard process of replacing fantasy with reality, there is nothing—but *nothing*—like time.

When we are young, it's nearly impossible for us not to have extreme ideas about all the wonderful things we're going to be someday, and all the wonderful *ways* we're going to be someday. Because when young, your whole life is nothing but pure, open-ended potential, a horizon-wide movie screen upon which you cannot help but project anything and everything you could ever want to do, know, and be.

It's very exciting! As the ebulliently naive Buzz Lightyear puts it in *Toy Story*, "To infinity—and beyond!"

By the time we reach middle-age, though, we're no longer living in a state of agitated anticipation of everything we can imagine our lives one day becoming. Because by then so much of our lives already *are* everything they could ever possibly be that we almost can't help but stop and wholly overhaul our understanding of just about everything having to do with ourselves and our lives. We do that because we now have in our grasp an unimaginably vast amount of evidence, knowledge, and experience that simply wasn't available to us back when one of our primary concerns in life was whether or not we'd know what to do the very first time we got kissed.

No one in middle-age has to wonder what the movie of their lives will be like. They've already fully lived half of that movie. They've *been* in that show. Even the person in middle-age who has realized their most cherished childhood dream—who actually *did* become an astronaut, or a famous singer, or the greatest athlete who ever lived—must at some point reckon with the difference between the dream they dreamed and the reality they've lived.

And if you gathered together the totality of everything that literally everyone in midlife has done and knows, what would be the singular most deep, true, and valuable of those things? If you are middle-aged, what's the biggest, most important, most life-changing, inspiring, exciting, gut wrenching, dangerous, mind-and-body blowing thing that you've ever done?

It's that you've loved.

You.

Have.

Loved.

And what that means (amongst all of the great many things that means) is that you know what true, deep, and inexhaustible compassion is.

Compassion! You have got it. You have used it. It has (alas—but love, as the song goes, hurts) used you.

You and compassion go way back. You know it so well because you know so well its nearest and dearest sibling, which is love.

For many, "Love yourself" feels like a fairly murky directive—consisting entirely, as it does, of arguably the two most loaded and complex words known to man. Which is why, instead of employing that phrase, I often find it useful to encourage people to show themselves compassion.

Just as I am encouraging you, right now, to feel for yourself the same compassion that you so easily and naturally feel for anyone you love. And then to feel it again. And then again. And again—for as long as it takes you to habitually grant yourself the same compassion that you habitually grant everyone you love.

Why should you hold yourself to a higher standard of worthiness or acceptability than you do other people? Why, if your child or your spouse burns a piece of toast, do you so readily say to them, "Don't feel bad. We have more bread. It's fine!", whereas if you yourself make the same mistake, you are wont take it as evidence, yet again, of what a stupid and inept loser you are.

Even if you don't put it to yourself in terms quite that harsh, you understand my meaning. If we could all learn to feel as kindly —as patient, as loving, as compassionate—toward ourselves as we do toward those whom we love, the world would be a much better place. And we would certainly feel much better in it.

THE YOU WHO'S LISTENING

Generally speaking, forgiveness follows an apology. It's a matter of exchange, a transactional dynamic.

It's a conversation, not a monologue.

That can present a bit of a problem when the person you're wanting to forgive is yourself. Because in that circumstance, who exactly is apologizing to whom? Who is supposed to forgive whom? The very idea of your forgiving you can quickly seem too solipsistic for words. Especially when it comes to forgiving yourself for the big stuff, the abiding transgressions, the deep wrongs we've all committed for which we are all too aware that a simple, "Forget about it; it's no problem" will hardly suffice.

Put another way: How do you forgive yourself when you *are* yourself? How can the criminal and the judge before whom he's pleading his case be the same person?

Who relieves their aching back by giving themselves a back

massage?

Inside of you, right now, is, and will forever remain, the little kid you used to be.

And that kid is a sweet kid. A good kid. A great kid: kind, open-hearted, always wanting what's best for everyone. A kid with boundless passion, limitless imagination, and all the love in the world.

That's who you were when you were a child. That's how all children are.

And then, as time went on, you couldn't help but become aware of that things around you were not nearly as simple as they had seemed to you before.

Slowly but surely—or quickly, if the home you were in was particularly dysfunctional—things for you got complicated. Maybe your mother was prone to falling into dark pits of depression. Maybe your father was gentle one moment, and filled with rage the next. Maybe you had a sibling who delighted in torturing you, or an uncle who had given you reason to tremble at the thought of being yet again left alone with them.

Maybe, due to any of the endless ways by which children come to feel threatened or insecure in their homes, you were afraid.

If so, then there was absolutely one thing which you had literally no choice but do to. And that was to change. Adjust. Adapt.

Survive.

Maybe, in order to at least increase your chances of surviving, you learned the value of pretending to feel—until perhaps you really did feel—callous, tough, inured from pain. Maybe you had to become as entertaining—as funny, as clever, as diverting—as you possibly could, since to keep 'em laughing is to keep 'em at bay. Maybe the role you adapted in your family was the ever-vigilant keeper of the peace: the rational voice, the calming influence, the dampener of storms. Maybe you became the tireless enabler, always running next door to borrow cigarettes for your mother, or to the liquor store to pick up a bottle for your father.

Whatever you needed to do in order to make it in your house is what you did. Whomever you needed to become in order to survive is who you became.

And it worked! You did it! You made it!

Congratulations for that, and I'm not kidding. It is no mean feat to make it to middle-age. Think of how many, for one reason or another, do not.

But you did. (I assume you did, anyway. Either that, or you so assiduously plan for the future that you're reading this book in anticipation of middle-age, in which case you are definitely a horse I would bet on.)

The good news is that you survived whatever dysfunctions in your family you had to.

The bad news is that that survival cost you something. It cost you something dear. It cost you something precious.

It cost you the little boy or girl you used to be.

You had to leave that kid behind. You had no choice but to. That kid was not prepared to make it in the world—and probably especially not in the world of your childhood home.

So somebody had to step in. Somebody had to take over.

Somebody had to protect that loving, trusting, exquisitely vulnerable child.

And that somebody was you.

You stood up. You directly faced everything in the world that came your way. You essentially told your inner child to stay in his or her bedroom or safe spot, and not to worry about a thing, because you would take care of everything. And then that's what you did. You started taking the hits, so that he or she wouldn't have to. And to handle those hits you did and became everything you needed to do and become.

And as that new person—as the person you had to become in order to protect the child you couldn't afford to be—you then went out into the world.

You went to school.

Eventually you left your home.

You started living your life.

And if you're like most people, in rushing to live that all-consuming life you left behind the child you had been.

The child who is still right where you last saw him or her, and who has been there ever since, patiently awaiting your return.

The child who has been there every second of every minute of your life. The child who has never stopped watching you, never stopped rooting for you, never stopped admiring you. Never, for a single moment, has your inner child stopped loving you.

How could they? You're their hero! You're the one who saved them! Of course your child will wait for you to return to him or her; they'll happily wait forever, if that's what it takes. They *love* you. They'd do anything for you.

And do you know what that "anything" includes?

It includes forgiving you.

Almost everything bad or wrong—or even just morally suspect —that you have ever done in your life you did for the exact same reason that anyone ever does anything bad, wrong, or morally suspect.

You were afraid.

That's it. No more; no less. There is no crime or wrongdoing that is not a response to fear.

Sure, you feel guilty for a whole world of things you've done in your life. Everybody feels that way. Some of your offenses are clear and easily (if painfully) recalled, others over the years became like threads which, through some dark force of their own, knitted themselves together into a kind of dysfunctional electric blanket that is always covering some if not all of your body, and is forever randomly zapping you with shocks of every intensity, from ones you barely feel at all to ones that bolt you suddenly upright in the middle of the night.

And all of your offenses—every mean or wrong thing you have ever said, thought, or done—you did out of fear.

Want to forgive yourself for one or all of the bad things you've ever done? Want to forgive yourself, even, for the person you are, for the person you became—or never became?

Then you have to return to the child you left behind.

Return to your inner child.

Be with that child. Hold that child. Hug that child. Feel while that child hugs you back until his or her arms are exhausted.

Talk to that child. Tell that child all that you've been doing with your life since last the two of you were together.

Finally, apologize to him or her.

Apologize for leaving them behind, and for not checking in often enough to ask them how they're doing.

Apologize for becoming everything you've become, and for doing everything you have ever done, which might have been any sort of betrayal of them: of what they believe in, care about, know to be true.

Just apologize. For all of it.

And I promise you this: Your inner child will instantly, thoroughly, utterly and breathlessly forgive you for anything you've ever done, no matter how wrong or bad.

Of course they will! They love you. They admire you. They think you're amazingly and unspeakably awesome.

And you better believe that they know perfectly well how much you've sacrificed trying to keep the wolves of the world away from their door.

Which you did.

And let them now thank you for that. Let them show you all the love and appreciation they've been feeling for you all of this time.

While it might seem daunting or even overwhelming, forgiving yourself, when it comes right down to it, is as easy as getting hugged by a child.

CHAPTER 4: CONFIDENCE
THE BIG PICTURE

Having opened the boxes labeled *Forgiving others* and *Forgiving yourself,* you approach the next box. Looking at its gift tag, you read the word *Confidence.*

You lift the box's lid, and peer inside.

What you see there is (and I'll have to ask you to please bear with me on this) a giant camera obscura—which is typically a small building.

I want you to enter this giant camera obscura. You'll have to shrink down far enough to make that possible—but I'm sure you won't mind.

Stepping inside, you find yourself in a large dark room. Taking up nearly the whole of the room's floor is a large reflective disc. You step up to the railing that runs around the disc, and look down at it.

If you have ever been inside an actual giant camera obscura, you know that what mini-you would see on that disc is a live, 360 degree view of whatever was happening for maybe a mile around the building. It is for this reason that giant camera obscuras are usually built on locations offering a spectacular view—high on a point that looks out over the ocean, for instance, or across a beautiful mountain range.

If you've never been to a camera obscura, I encourage you to visit one if you ever get the chance. It's a wonderfully eerie experience, gazing from what feels like the great beyond down onto a vast view of the world you've never had before. It's especially riveting if you are looking at a scene with people in it—people walking along the beach, for instance, or strolling through a field or garden.

The room is perfectly quiet. The people you are looking down upon are silently standing and admiring the view, or strolling along, alone or holding hands with their partners; the ocean waves are silently crashing, the wind is silently moving through the tops of the trees. And it all seems to be happening in this lovely, almost slow-motion, perfectly coordinated orchestration of movement.

Viewing the world in this way really is an other-worldly experience. It's how you imagine the world must appear to an angel up in heaven looking down upon it through an opening in the clouds.

Except, this particular camera obscura is different from any other.

This one is not overlooking the ocean or mountains.

This one is overlooking—is showing you—the whole of your life.

Standing at that railing, peering down at the disc, you see yourself as a child, playing with one of your favorite toys, or contentedly hiding from the world in that special little spot you always went to, the one that nobody in the world knew about but you.

There you are, running about with your friends. Riding your bicycle along with them. Walking with them to school.

Being with that favorite pet of yours, the one you loved so dearly.

Sharing your first real kiss with your first true love.

On that great soundless viewing surface you see your parents, holding you, loving you, scolding you, surprising you, rewarding you, amazing you, disappointing you. Saying hello to you. Saying good-bye.

You see your siblings.

Your spouse.

Your children.

Your boss from one job, your co-workers from another.

And always you, you, you, navigating through it all.

Growing. Striving. Thriving. Trying. Wanting. Needing. Being buckled by fear and empowered by need. Getting what you want, wanting what you don't.

Making promises you swear you'll keep forever.

Breaking promises that you always knew you would.

Hurting.

Being hurt.

All of it.

I am asking you to please, right now, in real time, take a moment or ten, and, insofar as you can, hold in your mind and heart the totality of your life.

See, please, the movie (or at least the highlight reel) of your life.

THE PAST ISN'T PAST

I ask you to hold in your mind's eye as much of your life as you can, because I know what a vital exercise that can be generally, and especially for a person who is either unhappy in their life, or is facing challenges which they find particularly daunting.

Why is this such a valuable exercise? Because we tend, very much, to view our lives linearly, as if they happen in a direct line, from the moment of our birth straight through until we die. And of course it's natural to see our lives in this way; we do, after all, live from one moment to the next, have one experience after the other, as if we are walking down a road (however winding, rocky, or steep that road might be).

But, as much as anything else, the idea that we live our lives linearly is an illusion, a trick of perception. In reality our lives are more like ripples of water spreading out in a pond. We are at the center of those ripples. We are the point of impact upon the water of our lives.

William Faulkner wrote, "The past isn't dead. It isn't even past." It is this phenomenon to which he was referring, this truth that we are always, to whatever degree we're aware of it at any given moment, experiencing our present amidst the totality of our past.

At no point in our life is this fact more important for us to grasp than it is in midlife. Because it is in midlife that we are very definitely facing challenges for which most of us are, or at least feel that we are, unprepared.

There is our home, feeling like an empty nest.

There is our career, feeling spent.

There are we, feeling old.

There is our death, feeling a good deal closer than it used to.

There, mainly, is the rest of our life, feeling like shadowy and unknown territory.

And with what armor can we gird ourselves as we step into this unknown territory? What weapons can we take up to bring along with us? From whence the resources necessary to assure that we survive (let alone thrive) in this daunting new land?

That, right there, is the easiest question in the world to answer.

We take with us all of our history.

But it's more than that. It's more specific than that, more refined, more pointed.

What we actually take with us is our *perception* of our history.

None of us really knows what all happened to us in our past; we can't possibly know all of the stories behind of the events that ultimately affected us.

All we know is how we feel in, and about, the present.

And how we feel in and about the present tends to be the cumulative effect of how we feel about our past—that is, how we feel about what *happened* to us in the past.

Especially—and perhaps even exclusively—how we feel, and how we felt, about the people and events in our lives that have always meant the most to us.

Which brings us right back into the home in which we grew up, doesn't it?

It brings us face to face with our parents.

About parents, Kahlil Gibran wrote, "You are the bows from which your children as living arrows are sent forth."

It is in midlife that the arrow we are hits the top of its long arc, and is then finally on its way to being firmly grounded.

THE REGULAR KIND

Life is hard. And it's hard for everyone: rich man, poor man, beggar man, thief. No one, as they say, rides for free.

And what a shame that is! Because it would have been fantastic if life had been nothing but a bowl of cherries for your parents.

And for my parents. And for everyone's parents.

And maybe, for some people's parents, it was. Maybe some people's parents somewhere managed to grow up to become happy, kind, and thoughtful people who never did or said anything that ever made their own children feel anything but good and positive about themselves and the world.

Boy, wouldn't it have been great to have had *those* parents?

Somebody, somewhere, must have. Such parents must exist *somewhere* out in the world, right?

Right?

Right?

Hello?

Well, I can promise you that the moment I personally meet anyone who had such parents—or even anyone who thinks they *know* someone who had such parents—I will let you know.

And you promise to do the same, okay? Because I want to meet those parents—and certainly the children they raised.

But until that day arrives, you and I shall only ever know (and be) people who had the other sort of parents.

The kind that are more difficult to have.

The kind who weren't geniuses at healthy parenting.

The flawed kind.

The regular kind.

The human kind.

The kind of parents who, whether purposefully or thoughtlessly, whether cruelly or stupidly, whether a little all the time or a lot at random times, instilled in their children what amounts to the fear that life can never really be good, can never really be fair, can never really be something that won't, at a moment's notice, turn bad.

Who taught their children that life can never really be trusted to be good.

I chose a profession which daily brings me into the deep inner lives of people from every walk of life who had parents who instilled in them such fears.

Which is not to say that the people who come to me for counseling do so consciously aware that they are harboring those fears. Of course they don't. For they, like all of us do, long ago learned to deal with those fears by covering them up, denying them, ignoring them, trying to forget them.

All they know, by the time they come to me, is that something has gone wrong with their lives. That they're not happy. That they're so unhappy they're hurting themselves and the people they love.

Something inside of them is broken, and they don't know what it is.

So, together, they and I get busy discovering what it is.

And what it almost always turns out to be—or what, at the very least, usually figures heavily as a component of whatever it ultimately became—is that, when they were children, their mother and/or their father instilled in them, at the deepest levels of their consciousness, indelible feelings of insecurity. Of inadequacy.

Of fear.

And what kind of an adult does a child who has wired into their psychological DNA fear and insecurity grow up to be?

But of course: one who lacks—whether they know it or not, whether they're ready to allow themselves to know it or not—confidence.

Confidence that they can always make themselves be safe.

Confidence that they are trustworthy.

Confidence that they are good.

Confidence that they are a person who deserves to be loved.

SOMETHING FROM NOTHING

When Willem was but an infant, his father started hitting him. And then he kept hitting him.

It got so bad that friends and neighbors of Willem's mother contacted child protection services in their area, and the agency sent out a case worker to assess the situation in Willem's home.

What that person found was so bad that she immediately, on the spot, removed Willem from the home. This was, to say the least, an unusual action for child protection services to take, so you can imagine how disturbing what the agent found must have been.

Forty or so years later, when Willem came into my office for the first time, he didn't even remember that that had happened to him. He didn't learn of just how bad his infant-hood was until (and while he was in therapy with me) he got hold of some official records which informed him about this terrible trauma from the very first months of his life.

What he did have some memories of was the home in which the child protection services agency placed him after removing him from his original home. He lived in that home for the next four years.

"I don't remember a whole lot from that time," he told me. "But what I do remember isn't . . . well, it isn't good. The lady who I thought of as my mom used to put me in this closet that was in the hallway of the house. I don't know why she did it, or what I might have done to cause her to do it. All I remember is this look that she'd get on her face—this really angry, crazy look—and then she'd come after me. I'd try to run away, or whatever, but, you know, I wasn't exactly a track star at the time. And I just re-member her hand slamming down on the back of whatever shirt I was wearing—or her gripping me hard by my upper arm—and basically just picking me up and dragging me to the closet. She'd open the door, throw me in, slam the door shut, and that would be that."

Willem looked down at his lap, as if embarrassed to be relating what he was. "The door wasn't locked. But I knew that if I opened it, and tried to leave the closet, she'd find me real fast and start hitting me. She used to hit me with clothes hangers. And that was worse than sitting in the dark in the closet. So I'd just stay there.

"Besides the fact of never being able to see anything in there, what I remember most about being in that closet were the shoes and boots on the floor in there. I hated those things. They always hurt the most when she tossed me in there, and were always what I had to deal with as I tried to clear a little place for me to sit down. They just always seemed to me to be nothing but sharp heels and toes.

"I remember sitting in the closet for so long I used to lie down in there. I'd reach up and start feeling around for the coats in there, because one of the coats, which I guess belonged to my mom—was, like, a fur coat, or a fake one, I'm sure, because I don't think they had any more money than my real parents did, which was basically none. But that coat was real soft. So I'd keep feeling through all the coats and sweaters up there till I found that one, and then I'd get to my feet, and as quietly as I could possibly manage take it off of its hanger, and bring it down on the floor with me. And I'd arrange it down there, and push all the shoes and boots to one side of the closet, and make a little nest out of the coat to lie down in.

"I remember just lying there, staring at the crack of light under the door, and wishing so hard that I was small enough to run underneath the door and get away. It used to make me really happy to think of her seeing me running across the floor, and it making her jump up on the coffee table and screaming. I think that's why I used to love mice so much when I was a kid."

Willem had a few other memories of life in that home. He remembered that for dinner he used to get served grape jelly. He remembered his "father" making him stand in the bathroom with him while he sat on the toilet. He remembered a time when his "mother" once dragged him out into the family backyard, made him strep naked, and then sprayed him all over with a hose.

"Maybe I peed myself, or something," said Willem. "I don't remember. I just remember how cold that water was. I thought I was going to die."

When Willem was four or five years old, his biological mother, who by then had left Willem's father, managed to regain custody of her son.

About a year after Willem moved back in with her, guess whom his mother brought back into her life?

And back into her house?

But of course: Willem's biological father. A man who, from that point on, Willem very definitely remembers.

The good news, such as it is, is that Willem's father didn't beat Willem as ferociously as he had when Willem was a baby.

The bad news is that he still hit him. A lot. He was just more careful about how he did it.

Now he knew how to hit the boy so that it didn't leave any marks—or so that the marks and bruises it did leave would always be hidden by Willem's clothes.

When Willem was fifteen years old, he ran away from home.

Now here's the thing about Willem: he is smart. Not just regular-person smart, but genius smart. And what he is smart at is mathematics. He's just one of those people for whom analytical logarithms and calculus formulas come as easily as driving a car does for most people.

He's also a powerful physical presence. Looking at Willem, just about the last thing even the most pugnacious person would think to do is to engage him in any sort of physical altercation. He is tall, broad-shouldered, and thick. Not fat. Thick. Solid. Like a really big fire hydrant.

It is a testimony to Willem's inner strength that he finished both high school and college. And he didn't just finish his formal education, either; he shined throughout it. He was a star pupil. In the summer between his freshman and sophomore years in college, Willem got married. Soon thereafter he had his first child, a son.

So throughout Willem's college career, he took classes full-time and also worked forty-hours a week at a grocery store.

"How did you do all of that?" I once asked him. "When did you sleep?"

"I didn't," he said tersely. I believed him.

When I met him, Willem said most of the things he said tersely. He seemed burdened by a heavy emotional weight that he appeared to just accept, however grimly, as simply part of being alive. You could tell that heaviness, that burden, was something that had been with him his whole life. It was part of the bones of his being.

By the time he graduated with a master's degree in mathematics, Willem had been married for nearly six years, and he and his wife had two sons. So great at math was he, that upon graduation he was offered a professorship in the mathematics department of the university where he'd earned his master's. He was offered a similar position at other colleges.

He turned those down.

After living for six long years as a poor married college student —and as a poor high school student for four tough years before that, and a poor kid for all his life before that—Willem wanted some money. And he was finally in a position to earn some.

So he took a job at one of the largest tax accounting firms in the world.

And he didn't join the firm as an entry level employee, either. He joined as someone whom the firm wanted to be sure would not be tempted to take a position anywhere else.

By the time he was thirty-five, Willem was a partner in that firm, and he and his wife were, by just about any standard, wealthy.

Five years after that, when Willem came to me, he was having something near a full-blown midlife crisis. He was estranged from his sons. He was acting out in sexual ways that were endangering his marriage and his career. He had started, for the first time in his life, to drink.

And Willem wasn't the type of person to do anything he did in a small or modest way. So when he started drinking, a lot of bottles started showing up in his outdoor garbage bin.

His life—his brilliant life, which he had so painstakingly scratched together for himself from materials as raw as raw gets—was coming unraveled.

He had finally made it to the top.

And from there he was tumbling down.

My guess is that no one who knew Willem (with the possible exception of his wife) would have ever said of him that he lacked confidence. That just wasn't something that seemed to be a part of who he was. The man was physically imposing, blazingly smart, almost aggressively gregarious (if that's what was called for), and extremely successful professionally.

How could such a man possibly lack confidence?

Of course, you know exactly how. You get a man with no confidence—no matter what he's managed to do with his life, no matter who or how he might seem to be—when you regularly beat him as a baby. Or as a child. Or as a teen. Or ever.

You beat a child, and, as naturally as the night follows day, that child comes to believe that they *should* be beaten, that they deserve to be beaten, that getting beaten is, and always will be, their fate.

It didn't matter that Willem had become the man he had. Because, at his very core, he had never stopped being the child he had been.

He had, in fact, spent his whole life running from that child.

He didn't want to know that child. He didn't want to remember that child.

He sure as heck didn't want to be that child.

And so he had turned his life into everything it had become.

And then he turned on it.

OUT WITH THE OLD

Men such as Willem are typically disinclined to admit they need help—and are usually repelled by the entire notion of seeking out help for their psychological problems. They feel this way because getting to the bottom of one's psychological problems necessarily involves looking back at one's past. And men (and women, to be sure) who are driven as Willem is do not like to backwards. They want to look forward. They want to keep going. They want to keep fighting.

But here's the thing about the past: Faulkner was right. There is no such thing. The past is always present. And if you try to pretend that it's not, if you try to pretend that you are no longer living in the aftermath of your childhood—and especially if that childhood was in any way difficult or traumatic—then sooner or later your past is going to come destructively sweeping into your present, whether you recognize it at the time for what it is or not.

The water that you've been trying to keep dammed up behind you all of your life will start to leak. There are few guarantees in life as certain as that. And, just as surely, ignoring that leak for too long will mean the breaking of that dam.

And then there you'll be, swimming in that old, dirty, toxic water again.

Willem started seeing me because his wife insisted upon it. The choice she gave him was as simple as it was non-negotiable: he could either get psychological counseling to address whatever it was inside of him that seemed to be winning its war against him; or he could leave her, and go fight his demons on his own somewhere.

Willem didn't want to lose his wife and sons. So he and I began working together.

And when I tell you what I discovered about Willem—or, more accurately, what I helped Willem to discover about himself—will come as no surprise to you.

We found that he was angry.

Of course he was! He'd been regularly beaten to within an inch of his life before he was old enough to climb out of his crib—and then sent to live with a foster "family" that wasn't qualified to take care of a houseplant, let alone a severely traumatized child. Then he spent his boyhood living in abject terror actually *relieved* by his father's agonizing physical abuse, since at least that abuse broke, for however short a time, the unbearable anticipation that is waiting for yet another beating.

And then there was his biological mother, who was forever frenziedly hugging and clasping Willem, crying about how much she hated to see him suffering.

So, yeah, Willem was mad.

But saying that Willem was mad is like saying the sky is big. It does state the fact. But it doesn't quite capture the scale of the thing.

Willem's anger was like the water behind a dam that was never going to be strong enough to contain it. Not forever, anyway.

But darn if that dam wasn't strong enough to hold that water back for as long as Willem needed it to.

It was strong enough to hold it back while he finished high school.

It was strong enough to hold it back while he finished college.

It was strong enough to hold it back while he spent years working so many hours at his firm that his co-workers nicknamed him Kronos, for the Greek god of all-devouring time.

It was strong enough to hold it back while Willem become a decent husband, father, and provider.

And then, when he no longer had anything left to fight or conquer, his dam started to crack. It started to leak.

Except, here's the thing. By the time Willem's pent-up anger started spilling over into his life, he had no idea of what was actually happening there. He was aware, of course, that he was growing increasingly, and even compulsively, angry, restless, and self-destructive. He just didn't know why. His anger was welling up from a source so deep inside of himself that he didn't even recognize that it was part and parcel of his own experience, that it was essentially a delayed reaction to his childhood. The very idea of that being true was as alien to him as would have been the suggestion that his problems were being beamed into his head him by an actual alien.

"To tell you the truth, Dr. Ana," he said to me, almost shyly, in one of our first counseling sessions. "I don't know what's happening to me. Maybe it's a vitamin deficiency or something. I don't know. All I know is that it's bad, and getting worse. Last night I was trying to thread the top of a plastic bottle onto the thing we have that makes carbonated water. I couldn't get the bottle to go on. And, in an instant, I was so angry that I hurled the full bottle of water *and* the soda-making thing across the kitchen, and into the living room, where they smashed against the wall maybe a foot away from a window. Nobody got hurt or anything. But my wife was sitting on the couch watching television when those things came sailing across the room. You should have seen the way she looked at me. I'll tell you one thing. I don't want to ever see that look on her face again. I can't be the guy who makes his wife look at him like that. Okay?"

"Okay," I said.

During the course of his therapy with me, Willem came to understand two seminally important things about himself. The first was that he was, in fact, almost unimaginably angry about his childhood.

The second was that his being almost unimaginably angry about his childhood was perfectly okay.

He learned that it was even more than okay. He learned that it was good. He learned that the burning anger and helpless depression that had been burned into him as a child was an entirely reasonable and natural response to what was being done to him at the time.

With patience and careful guidance, Willem came to understand and appreciate that, far from compromising the quality of his life—far from being his enemy—his deep and abiding anger had saved him. Not *all* of his childhood anger had been pushed back behind the dam. As much of it as he could contain within himself and still remain functional had always been with him.

That anger—which he didn't even *recognize* as such, since it and fear—the other side of anger's coin—were just about the only emotions he had ever experienced as a child—had always been Willem's weapon. It had always been his shield. It had always been the force that served to separate him from the reality of the nightmare he was living through.

Anger is what gave Willem his focus, his drive, the almost detached determination he needed in order to accomplish all that he had. Anger was the fuel that drove him as far away from his childhood as he could possibly get.

And then Willem kept on driving, right up to middle-age.

And what happened to him then is what happens—or what should happen—to pretty much anyone who reaches middle-age.

He learned that the defense mechanism upon which he had relied to get him through his childhood was now working against him. The anger that had fueled his rocket as a boy and younger man was now burning up his life.

Willem was like a man in prison who spends twenty years using a metal spoon to dig himself out of his cell—and who then, once free and out in the world, keeps compulsively scraping his spoon against everything and everyone he meets.

His tool worked when he needed it to. But because it did, he doesn't need it anymore. He just has to realize that.

STILL STANDING

Middle-age is the time when we all get to recalibrate, or even wholly refashion if that's what we want, everything about how we relate to ourselves, the world, and everyone in it.

As children, most (if not all) of us instinctively pulled forth from our inner selves an array of defensive mechanisms—or, as in Willem's case, just one big one—that we used to survive whatever dysfunctional dynamics were prevalent in our home. Some of us learned to strategically and habitually withdraw; others to unfailingly defer and accommodate; others to be uproariously funny—or studious, or irresponsible, or sexy.

We became who we needed to be in order to get through what we needed to get through.

And good for us! I think every person in the world who is forty-five years or older should wear a huge badge all the time that says, "I'm still here!" Or, "Take THAT, my childhood!" *Something* which indicates that they're aware that the period of their life which is unquestionably the most difficult and challenging is now in their past.

Except not every person in midlife feels that way, do they? Certainly the ones in midlife who come to see me aren't generally feeling that way. They're usually feeling as if *now* is the most difficult their life has ever been.

And why do they feel that way? Because usually what they're doing is what they've always done, which is to relate to the world and themselves from within the same emotional and psychological framework they did when they were children. They're coming from the only place they've ever come from. They're reacting in the only way they've ever reacted.

They're still using their spoons.

What they're doing is being the same person they've always been. Because what other person *could* they be? How could they have ever learned, as children, to do and be anything different, when they learned what to do and how to be—and how to save and protect themselves—before they had anywhere near the wherewithal to know that there were any other options available to them?

You don't *choose* a persona. You pick up the first one that fits. All children do that—and in so doing, in many ways set themselves for life. They fully become what they need to become in order to maximize their fortunes within the family into which they were born—and then naturally and fully *stay* with that, as if their lives depended upon it. Because they very often have reason to feel that it just might.

And then, wearing that same cloak which protected or inured them during their childhood, they go out into the world.

And they do their thing. They grow. They develop. They learn.

And at some point along the way, they find themselves feeling painfully constrained. Cramped. Uncomfortable in the life they've made for themselves.

Why? Because they've outgrown that cloak. It doesn't work any more. It's not helping anymore.

And in that very real sense, that *is* making their life the worst it's ever been. Because at least the cloak they're still wearing used to fit. At least it used to be helpful. At least it worked.

Now it doesn't. Now wearing that same old cloak is all too often making them at the very least appear, they know, the fool.

But without that cloak, they fear that they will be too stripped to protect themselves. Without their cloak, they're afraid, at their most primitive level, that they will be naked, vulnerable, ripe to be slaughtered.

And they would be. They would be, that is, except for one phenomenal, liberating, paradigm-shattering fact:

They are not children anymore.

And they haven't been children for a long, long time.

They haven't been children in so long, in fact, that, if they but think about it—if they only allow themselves to acknowledge and accept it—they will see that, by any measure, they have now acquired for themselves enough knowledge, experience—and, yes, enough wisdom—to rip their tired, useless old cloak right off their shoulders, and don in its place anything that they might care to wear.

Being able to do that—knowing that changing is the next logical thing *to* do—is the very singular gift of middle age. That's the gift of going into the camera obscura, of holding and seeing in your mind everything you've ever fought against, everything that's ever tried and failed to knock you out, everything you've ever done which proved, beyond a doubt, that you are one formidable survivor.

There are a lot of things that mid-life cannot bring you. But one of those things is not confidence.

If you're in midlife, then the very fact that you are means that confidence is yours for the taking.

And I'm not talking about the kind of confidence that evokes braggadocio, or bold and brilliant people doing bold and brilliant things because they know perfectly well that they're too bold and brilliant to fail. I'm not talking about the hollow confidence of the accomplished showboat.

It's not even talking about the confidence of knowing that you can do anything.

It's even deeper than that.

I'm talking about the confidence of knowing that you can *try* anything—and be perfectly fine, whether you fail at it or not.

I'm talking about the confidence born of knowing that, *simply by virtue of having been alive for four or five decades,* you have collected and generated enough moments of strength—and of intelligence, and of kindness, and of toughness, and of sacrifice, and of all the kinds of powers that come from making all the kinds of mistakes that you have—not to have to worry anymore about whether or not it's okay for you to be happy.

I'm talking about the confidence that comes from knowing, in your heart of hearts, that it *is* okay for you to be happy, and peaceful.

And the proof of that being true is that you're still here.

You've *earned* the right to be happy and peaceful and confident.

And no one can take that away from you. No one can make you un-live the life you've lived, un-know everything you know.

You've won. You've got this.

You've got all of it.

In his song, "I'm Still Standing," Elton John sings these words:

I'm still standing, better than I ever did

Looking like a true survivor,

feeling like a little kid.

I couldn't have said it better myself.

CHAPTER 5: CREATIVITY

And which of the seven gifts waiting for you in the great passageway of midlife do you next approach?

The one marked (as you discover by reading its gift tag) *Creativity.*

As a schoolgirl, one of my teachers used to keep in our classroom, along with all the other supplies we used for our arts and crafts project, a color wheel. A disc as large as a hubcap, it showed all the colors in existence—or at least the main ones, and a great many of their shades. It comprised two wheels, each with countless colors streaming out from the little white button which kept them together at their center. You turned the top wheel, and through a variety of windows saw through to the colors on the wheel below. In this way did I learn about the relationships between primary colors, complimentary colors, secondary colors, tertiary colors, and so on.

I adored that wheel. I could get lost for hours in its endless array of brilliant possibilities. Sometimes, while the other kids ran outside for recess, I would stay inside the classroom for a little bit longer, just so I could spend some more time slowly turning and lingering over that wonderful wheel.

So. You might not be surprised to learn that the gift you find inside the box *Creativity* is . . . your very own color wheel!

It would be easy to suggest that in middle age one should allow oneself to become an artist—that is, to enthusiastically explore one's naturally artistic side. One of the reasons that assertion would be so easy to make is because it is absolutely, one hundred percent true. And, make no mistake, I will most ardently be making that very suggestion below.

Before we get to that, though, I want to take a moment to talk about the fundamental problem with the general advice, "Become an artist!". Namely, that statement assumes that by the word "art" we mean exclusively the creative arts: painting, sculpture, dance, etc.

All of which are wonderful, and all of which I believe any person would benefit from doing. There's not a person in this world whose outlook on life wouldn't immediately start improving if they started doing a creative art. That's just a fundamental truth of being human. We do all love to paint, to sing, to sink our fingers into moist clay and start shaping it into whatever we feel like shaping it into. It's not a mystery as to why the makers of cell phones continuously strive to improve the camera on their phones. They know how much people enjoy taking photographs. And not just photographs of the fun things they and their friends and family are doing, but photographs that amount to art: pictures of sunsets, of bucolic or chaotic scenes, of intricate patterns of shadows and forms. It's all art. And it's all so much fun to create.

But there's a different kind of art to which I am also referring when I prescribe to anyone in midlife that they take advantage of what life is affording them at this phase of their life by opening themselves up to leading a more artistic life.

Yes, sometimes, that does indeed mean that they should start painting, writing, dancing, and so on.

But sometimes it means making the sort of change in their life that a client of mine once made in hers.

CLAUDETTE

Claudette was an industrial psychologist. She was someone whom corporations would hire to come in and speak to their employees as a group, thereby boosting staff moral, sharpening employees' sense of purpose, or inspiring personnel to think of ways in which they, or their company generally, could improve their processes or methodologies.

When the troops were down, or needed what she called "a good juicing up," Claudette was the person you called.

Over the years enough people had called Claudette, and found what she did so utterly worth what they paid her to do it, that, by the time I met her, Claudette's company consisted of herself and a dozen other professionals trained in the way she was.

Why had Claudette come to see me? Because she was suffering, in part, from what so many people in midlife are, which is the heavy and persistent malaise which sometimes comes from having professionally met one's career goals.

It's one thing—and no mean thing, to be sure! —to work and work and scrape and work some more, for years that turn into decades, until you have succeeded in your chosen profession.

It's another thing to know what to do with yourself next.

A friend of mine once trained for years in preparation for climbing one of the highest mountains in the world. Once he got up to the top of the mountain—and after his rush of adrenaline had subsided—he found himself first thinking, and then fairly consumed by, a thought which he'd never imagined would occur to him once he'd finally made it up there: Now what?

"It's really just the weirdest thing," Claudette said to me, early on in our meetings together. "But I'm somehow feeling two things, which should be the opposite of each other, but I guess aren't entirely. On the one hand, I'm feeling quite restless. Don't get me wrong: I love what I do. Seeing people's eyes as they light up, suddenly alive in their jobs again, is just so rewarding and exciting. But lately I feel like *I* need to show up to one of my inspirational speeches, like I need to feel inspired about *my* work again."

"That sounds like something worth exploring," I said.

Claudette smiled. "I *do* give a good talk. Except, I have to say, I think I'm beyond being inspired about inspiring others. I just feel like that whole huge chapter of my life—that whole first *half* of my life—has ended. Which, in a way, I'm okay with. The company is successful enough without me that I don't really need to be a part of its daily operation anymore; I can make a pretty good living now without ever showing up at work at all. So I'm kind of ready to move on. But I don't know to what. I feel like a dog who's been chained to a post all of its life, and suddenly the chain breaks. I'm free! Hallelujah! But then I just feel stuck, right there where I've always been, because I just don't know where to go with all my new freedom."

Because I'm aware of how often it proves invaluable in helping people to understand their present and their future, in the course of our sessions I encouraged Claudette to talk to me about her past. In particular I asked her to share with me things that, when she was a young girl, it had made her happy to think about, or to do.

At one point Claudette began telling me how much she used to enjoy babysitting. Apparently—and not that surprisingly, frankly, given Claudette—as a young teen she was quite the babysitting queen of her neighborhood. Many parents trusted her to look after their young children while they were away.

It was when she began to talk to me about this one family in her neighborhood that I saw in Claudette's eyes—and in her tone, and her body language—what I tend to look for when I'm listening to my clients talk about their childhoods.

She came alive, essentially. There was a spark. She sat up a little straighter. Her voice became slightly higher in pitch. I could just see that this was something she was excited about, all these many years later.

It seemed that in this family was a special needs child, a girl of nine years old who had Down syndrome.

"Her name was Mona," said Claudette. "I never really babysat her—or never for very long, anyway. I babysat for a couple of kids who lived next door to Mona's house, and those kids' mother was friends with Mona's mother. And so sometimes Mona and her mom, and her brother and sister, would come over when I was babysitting next door. And we'd all just hang out and play together, or whatever. It was fun.

"And I just always loved Mona so much. In fact, later on, when I was in high school, they opened up a school for special needs kids not too far from my school. The administrators of my school asked our teachers if they knew of any students who might be interested in assisting at the new special needs school. When one of my teachers asked the class if anyone was interested in volunteering for that work, I thought of Mona, and shot my hand right up.

"For the rest of that school year, I worked about ten hours a week at that school. And I loved it." Here Claudette got a kind of far away look in her eyes. "I was really good at helping the kids at that school do art. I don't really know why; I didn't do anything special or anything. But I remember somehow being really aware of the fact that it wasn't helpful to the students to in any way evaluate their art. One time there was this other volunteer, a girl like me from my high school, and she was with the class I was regularly assigned to one day when we were doing art. And I remember she was with a boy, a student, who was sitting next to the girl I was helping—and her saying to the boy something about what he could do to make the picture he was doing better— like maybe he should, you know, paint the sun yellow instead of purple, or something like that.

"And I remember thinking, 'No, no. That's wrong. Don't tell him that. Let him have fun. We're not entering these paintings in any kind of realism contest. If he wants a purple sun, let him have a purple sun.'

"And it really broke my heart, because when the boy heard what she said, he just deflated. He just slumped. Like he knew he was never going to be any good at painting, so he shouldn't even try." A tear came to Claudette's eyes. "That just killed me," she said.

I imagine you have a good idea of where this story is going, so I'll go ahead and get there. During the time that she and I were doing sessions together, Claudette started working, as a part-time volunteer and then a full-time paid assistant, at a school for special needs children. She found the work so rewarding that she returned to college, and earned a degree in special education. She's been working as a special needs teacher ever since.

ART WITH A CAPITAL "A."

The reason I wanted to share Claudette's story is because I know how common it is for people in middle age—especially if they're at or near the age of retirement—to hear, or be told, that it's a great idea for them, at that stage of their lives, to discover and/or embrace their creative selves. And that *is* a great idea, and we'll talk specifically about that below.

But before we do, I wanted to use Claudette's story to illustrate how, for some people, it's more about *thinking* creatively about their lives—it's about actually and creatively recasting their lives —than it is about picking up a songbook or a paintbrush.

Claudette's life didn't necessarily become any more objectively creative as a special education teacher than it had been when she was an inspirational speaker. It's that for *her* it was more creative. For *her* being a special education teacher had more of the raw material of life to it than did speaking to corporate groups. For *her* the change of career was the claiming of something deep, vibrant, and soul-nourishing that she realized she wanted for herself.

In Claudette's new life, she was, in fact, leading the life of an artist. It's just that instead of paint, a stage, or a piece of blank paper, the medium in which she was working was life itself. Her fresh and blank canvas was every single new day before her. The artistry of her life was revealed in the way she interacted with the children she taught. It was in how she responded to their needs. It was the manner in which she treated the young people whose lives were enriched by the power of her love for them.

So the gift of creativity isn't simply about opening up yourself enough to allow yourself to express yourself through an artistic medium. It can be about that, most certainly—and when it is about that, beautiful healing and joyous being almost can't help but happen. And we'll talk about that next. I just wanted to be sure that before we moved into discussing the value—and,

I would argue, the near indispensable value—of embracing the doing of the creative arts in middle-age, we took care to understand that, by art, we mean Art with a capital "A."

Besides doing creative work, we can mean—or, ideally, also mean—living creatively. We can mean living with the conscious understanding that every moment of our lives is a genuinely artistic opportunity for us, in that we can make of that moment—we can create of that moment—anything we might want it to be.

At this particular moment, in real time, you could suddenly start singing a song. You could start dancing. If you're sitting at a table in an open cafe, you could start moving around the objects on your table until you think they're placed in a perfectly beautiful pattern.

You could make something new out of the very next moment of your life.

And the amazing thing is, you *will* make something new out of the very next moment of your life. You don't have a choice in that. That's what being alive *is.*

We *move* into our futures; and the future, for every single one of us, is the very next moment of our lives. We decide what each new moment of our life is going to be—or what it's going to be and mean to *us,* anyway. And, let's face it: that's mainly what counts. How we feel about what we're doing and what is happening to us is what determines the actual day-in and day-out quality of our lives.

I can't control what the person next to me is thinking or doing. I can't make the person I'm talking to respond to what I'm saying in the way that I'd hoped or expected they would. That's not possible.

But what I *can* do is decide how I am going to feel about however that person responds to what I've said.

If their response to what I've said makes me angry, I can decide—right there, in that very moment—that I'm not going to be angry, after all. Instead of internally responding to them with something like, "You are so stupid; I can't believe you're not understanding what I'm saying to you!" I can think of how funny it is that, no matter how much we assume that everyone is just going to respond in the only way that it makes sense to *us* that they would, they almost never do.

That's a funny thing; you can enjoy that as a source of humor. If I choose that internal response over getting angry at the other person, I have just created a new moment for myself. My contention here is that that is *art.* It's taking something that is, in an almost absolute state, a certain way ("I've been offended; therefore, I am going to get angry") and from that *created* something unexpected, new, and beautiful.

Or, instead of getting angry at the other person for not properly hearing me, I might decide to listen to that person—and, in so doing, might hear, or realize, that they are suffering in some way that I certainly wouldn't have noticed, or been aware of, had I simply barreled ahead with my anger at how they responded to me.

And in that moment I would have created, in my very own heart, and almost out of nowhere, empathy.

That's art! That's living creatively! It's living every bit as creatively as anyone can. Creating a new and unexpectedly beautiful moment or feeling out of what, before that creation, held no promise of being anything different from what anyone would have expected it to be, is the very essence of art.

There's making art; and there's living artfully. And one isn't necessarily better than the other. They're just using different mediums.

All that said, let's now talk about the intrinsic and enduring, joys of making what most people think of when they think of the word "art."

MR. PAPER PLATE FACE

When I was a young teenager, the father of a friend of mine went through an extraordinary change. One sunny Saturday afternoon, as my friend and I were walking away from her house toward wherever it is was we were headed, I looked into her family garage through wide open door.

Inside the garage was my friend's father, whom I knew had very recently retired from his career as a police officer. He had built something, out of what appeared to be five boards and a paper plate.

He had built a person.

More specifically it was, basically, a stick-figure person: the kind young children draw, with a circle for a head, a line which comes straight down and then splits into an upside-down Y for the two legs, and two straight arms.

Only instead of a circle, this person's head was made of a paper plate, and instead of lines on a page, it was made out of pieces of wood.

On the paper plate—where the figure's face would be—my friend's dad had painted, in bright red, two crude eyes, a nose, and a great big smile. At the moment he was concentrating hard on, from what I could tell, attaching black yarn to the top of the plate. For, presumably, hair.

"What's your dad doing?" I whispered to my friend, looking over my shoulder at her father as we walked down the driveway.

My friend rolled her eyes, and with the exasperation with which, since time immemorial, teenagers have always talked about their parents, sighed, "I have no idea. He's been building those *people,* or whatever they are, ever since he retired. It's bizarre."

But I was instantly fascinated, and immediately started peppering my friend with questions. *"What?!* What are you *talking* about? *What* people? Like that one, you mean? How many of those has he built? Why is he doing it? Does he name them? Does he *do* anything with them? Is he building a whole *town* of them, you think? Where are the other ones? *Why is he doing that?"*

"I don't *know,"* said my friend, clearly baffled by my nearly maniacal interest in her father's apparently new passion. "Ask him if you want to know so much about what he's doing."

"I'm going to," I said. And I did—the very next day, in fact.

While my friend was inside the house eating her lunch, I nonchalantly made my way into the garage. There her father was working on the same board-person he'd been nailing together the day before. He was down on the ground, attaching an old pair of black men's shoes onto the bottom of the legs.

"Hi, Mr. Novak," I said.

He looked up from his shoe fitting, a big smile on his face. "Oh, hello there, Ana."

"Whatcha doin'?" I said casually.

He laughed. He was a giant of a man—tall and heavyset—and had a laugh to match his size. "Well, I'll tell you what I'm doing. I'm trying to put shoes on this fellow."

I nodded, as if I understood.

Looking at me a little mischievously, Mr. Novak said, "Do you think Hubert would wear shoes, Ana?"

"Hubert?"

"My friend here. That's his name."

"It is?"

Mr. Novak let out another laugh. "Well, I couldn't call him Mr. Paper Plate Face, could I?"

"No, I guess not," I said.

Mr. Novak seemed to grow a little thoughtful. Then, nodding pensively, he said, "I think Hubert would want shoes. How's he going to go walking around if he doesn't have any shoes?"

I spent the next half hour or so with Mr. Novak. I made some small talk with him, but all I really wanted to do was watch him, because I was still trying to answer for myself the question of why a grown man would want to spend his time making something that looked so, well, not worth making. What he had made looked like something _I_ could have made—with one hand tied behind my back.

But I knew Mr. Novak. He was a very long way from being a stupid man. I had always known him to be thoughtful, smart, kind, and generally pretty serious about things.

Yet here he was, nailing an ancient pair of shoes onto a six-foot-tall wooden stick-man with no hands, a paper plate for a head, and hair made of straggly black yarn that had been stapled to the top of his crudely drawn face.

Mr. Novak didn't seem to mind my being in the garage with him, so I took a seat on a tall stool at his workbench, and quietly watched as he carefully outfitted Hubert with shoes, and after that began fashioning hands for his creation out of tongue depressors.

After I'd been silently observing him for about ten minutes, I began to realize something quite extraordinary about Mr. Novak: he had forgotten I was there.

He was so absorbed in what he was doing that he had actually forgotten that there was a live human being there watching him do it. I could just see in his eyes, and read in his face, that he was absolutely oblivious to everything except the creation of Hubert.

And as I continued to watch the man work, I began to think about what it was that I found so fascinating about what I was seeing. I couldn't quite figure it out. What exactly was it about what was going on before me that I found so nearly mesmerizing?

And then it struck me.

The giant, grown, fully adult Mr. Novak was acting just like a kid. He was acting the way *I* had acted, back when I had been a kid playing with my dolls, coloring in my coloring book, or slowly turning that color wheel.

Mr. Novak was doing something that, as far as I knew, adults never, ever did.

He was playing.

He was doing something for the sheer pleasure of doing it.

"THINKING IT'S SERIOUS IS THE ONE SURE WAY TO RUIN IT."

Hubert—and the several proto-Huberts made before him—was only the beginning of Mr. Novak's artistic pursuits. Gradually, the oversized stick-people gave way to smaller, more realistic looking figures fashioned from paper mache—which, ultimately, gave way to figures made of sculptor's clay.

Within about five years, Mr. Novak was being recognized for the artist he had become. By the time I was a senior in high school, his sculptures were on display in quite a few public and private buildings around town.

One day his daughter and me drove with him to a local bank, in the lobby of which was one of his sculptures. When the bank had first unveiled the sculpture a month or so before, they had made a pretty big deal of it. There'd been a large reception attended by many civic luminaries, the local press and media had paid attention to the event, and so on. It all seemed to me a pretty big deal. Mr. Novak, the former police officer, was becoming famous as an artist.

En route to the bank, I asked Mr. Novak if it had been exciting to have gotten all the attention he did the night the bank revealed his stature.

He laughed. "Nah," he said.

"Really?" I said. "It didn't make you feel great?"

"I didn't let it make me feel great," he said.

This broke my brain a little bit. The idea of being publicly lauded for something you'd created *not* being a wonderfully rewarding experience was a concept just a bit too alien for my teenage mind to grasp.

I asked him to please explain what he meant.

Mr. Novak drove in silence for a while before saying the words of his that I've never forgotten, and expect I never will. "I do the art I do because I enjoy doing it," he said. "And that is the only reason I do it. If I let myself think that my art is great, or that I'm somehow special for doing it—or, even worse, that my art has any *meaning* beyond my simple doing of it—I'd quit doing it. Because then it wouldn't be fun anymore. In my opinion, when it comes to making art, *thinking it's serious is the one sure way to ruin it.*" (Emphasis mine.)

The reason I've never forgotten the words of Mr. Novak's which I've italicized above is because it's one of those rare things which becomes more true the more you reflect upon it.

This is an instance where thinking that something is serious makes that thing *better!*

More than any other time in a person's life besides during their adolescence, middle-age is a time of radical transformation.

The huge difference between the changes of adolescence and middle-age is that we can control the changes we go through in middle age. And, as I've said before, if we don't control those changes, they will control us.

So we want to be very clear about our goal in midlife: about what we want it to do *for* us, rather than to us.

And what I think the goal of midlife is—what I think is, or can be, its highest purpose—is that it allows you to gather together the totality of your life's experience—everything you've ever known, everything you've ever done, everything you've ever learned—and then to finally, for the first time in your life, *drop* all of it that doesn't serve any purpose anymore.

Midlife is the time of unburdening. Of shedding. Of releasing.

It's the time of reducing.

It's an opportunity—and more than an opportunity: it's a time when everything is finally exactly right for it—to get back to, or even for the first real time to discover—your true nature.

The core you.

The irreducible essence of who you are.

Midlife is an invitation to reconnect with who you were before the world started telling you whom you should be.

If you are in middle age, then up until this point in your life, you've been largely *reacting* to life.

You reacted to your parents. You reacted to your siblings. You reacted to your teachers, your friends, your jobs, your children ... you reacted to—you lived in response to—just about everything and everyone.

Which is all perfectly good and fine. It's how it should be. It's how it must be.

But now, in midlife, you're *done* with all of that. You've been influenced by everything that comprises the outside world just about as much as you need to be in order to finally be cognizant of who you most are on the inside.

You've been around the block—a few times.

Now it's time for you to come home.

Now, instead of being reactive to life, you can start being, with all the confidence in the world, proactive to life.

Because you've earned that. You've *learned* that. Just by virtue of the fact that you've been alive for as long as you have, you have, in one hard way or another, learned everything you need to know about how to be the happiest you that you can be.

Because now you know all the things that work for you, all the things that don't work for you, and all the things that used to work for you but don't anymore.

Now you know the wheat from the chaff.

And knowing that means you can now separate the two.

And that means good-bye, chaff.

Good-bye habits that don't work for you anymore.

Good-bye assumptions that don't work for you anymore.

Good-bye beliefs about yourself that don't work anymore.

Good-bye, all the extra baggage.

And once you have thrown out all of that chaff-heavy baggage—which you can do at a moment's notice, at the very second you decide for yourself that you can and will do that—do you know what you'll have left?

What you'll have left is you.

Your core nature.

Your fundamental self.

Your irreducible essence.

You'll have the true you.

And you know what the true you likes to do as much as he or she likes to do anything in this world?

Think back to that other time that you were your truest, most essential self.

Think back to when you were a kid.

I don't go out on any limb at all here when I say that I *know* that when you were a kid, you liked to do art.

You didn't think of it as "art," because "art" is serious, and serious is no fun. Mr. Novak was right about that.

You didn't care about art.

You cared about having fun.

You cared about doing stuff that really grabbed you. That absorbed you. That seemed to bring all of you into it, in a way few other things ever did.

You liked to paint. You liked to draw. You liked to dance. You liked to make things out of clay. You liked to build things that nobody but you really understood. You liked to write poetry or songs or funny little short stories.

And you probably liked doing one of those kinds of things more than you did the others.

You were a painter, a sculptor, a dancer, a musician.

When you were innocently, unpretentiously, and spontaneously being who you were—and when there was no one breathing over your shoulder about whether or not you were doing it "right"—you created.

You created because it was the purest and best kind of fun.

Well, it's time for you to have that fun once again in your life.

Life's just too short not to.

NO CRITICS ALLOWED

Art therapy—the phenomenon whereby a person, through doing art, is healed of their psychological malaise—works. I am always enthusiastic about starting or participating in art therapy, whether it be with an individual, or in a group setting, because I know that no one, no matter what condition they're in, or how bad they might be feeling, doesn't start feeling better—and then a lot better—once they start doing art.

And why is that so? Because through the doing of art, we connect with ourselves in a way that few if any other activities allow us to. There's just something about the doing of art that is so organic, so whole, so intrinsically integrating to all of the disparate energies that comprise the totality of the psychological matrix that defines us, that no one can do art and remain unchanged for the better.

Now, if that's true—and, not to overstate a point, but it absolutely is—then why do relatively so few adults ever do art? It's a curious thing, isn't it? If doing art is so much fun, and so richly enhances everything about our lives—if it's just so *great* a thing to do —then why don't more people do it?

It's as if, every single day, a person steps out of their front door, and then, first thing, takes one giant high step, in order to avoid tripping over the huge bag of gold that's sitting on their front porch.

Why wouldn't they just pick up that bag of gold? Why would they choose not to greatly enrich their lives, when doing so would be so, so easy?

Well, remember that special needs boy in Claudette's story who was told by someone who was basically an authority figure that the picture he was painting was somehow not up to snuff? That it wasn't quite right? That it wasn't really good enough?

Do you remember how that boy responded to that judgment of his creative work?

He stopped. In Claudette's words, he deflated.

He quit.

He was having good, organic, whole, true, spontaneous fun— he was *creating*—and then someone—someone who was in a position to know more about it than he did—judged his creation, and found it wanting.

And, just like that, that party shut down.

Now, to be clear, we shouldn't blame the teaching assistant who made whatever suggestion she did about how the boy might make his painting better. She was young and inexperienced; clearly no one had yet taught her that the surest way to eradicate the will to create in young people is to criticize any their creative efforts.

But, moreover, she was only doing what, at that point in her life, she could not possibly help but do. She was evaluating. She was assessing.

She was judging.

She was doing those things—she was making determinations about relative quality—because that is what humans *do.* It's what we all do. It's what we're all taught to do, from the very first moment that anyone in our lives (hello, mom and dad) rewards us for doing something that they clearly like us to do a whole lot better than they like us to do a whole bunch of other stuff we do.

If, as a baby, I learn that smiling at my mother will make her pet me and love me and give me food, then I will start smiling at my mother until my little baby cheeks ache.

Well, I might not go *that* far, but you get my meaning.

We learn what things are good, and what things are bad.

Playing with the dog's pooh? Bad. Sharing our toys with others? Good.

Pushing down a fellow playmate? Bad. Helping a fallen playmate back onto her feet? Good.

And on, and on, and on—judging, and learning or adapting new criteria for that judging—just about every moment of our waking lives.

We humans are, in short, a judging species. And not because we're bad people, or small-minded, or insecure, or anything like that. We judge because that's what our brains are wired to do. Our brains know the difference between all of the opposites: between good and bad, right and wrong, light and dark, hot and cold, yes and no, up and down, happy and sad—and, again, on and on and on.

We can't help what we know. And what we know is that everything is relative.

What we also know is that everything is not equal. Some things are manifestly better than other things. It's better not to have a broken leg than to have a broken leg. It's better not to freeze to death than it is to freeze to death. It's better to have the person you love you back, than it is to have them run over you with their car.

We humans are smart—smart enough to know enough to judge pretty much everything, anyway—and we are social. And all social creatures naturally, innately, and inevitably establish hier-archies of value.

And we could no sooner *not* apply to ourselves the judgments we apply to literally everything else in the world than we could not bend our knees when we sit down.

It's just not possible.

And here, again, we come to one of *the* great gifts of midlife.

Finally, we are able to actually stop judging ourselves.

It's not easy; it's a definite challenge to stop doing something we've been so automatically and even instinctively doing all day long, every day of our lives.

But we can do it. We can stop judging ourselves; at the very least, we can greatly reduce how often we do it.

And, oh my gosh, should we ever.

Think about it. At this point in your life, what possible good can come from your (continuing to) judge yourself? Will you learn anything new about yourself the next time you judge your-self? Will it help you at all to, one more time, call yourself fat, or dumb, or insecure?

Of course you won't.

Why? Because you are *past* all that now.

You've been down that road so often it's now officially a rut. A rut you can hop right out of.

It's hard, I know, to cease judging yourself altogether. We've all got tapes running through our heads, constantly pointing out to us all of the good and bad (and usually it's one good for every thousand bad) things about ourselves.

But there is one place where you can, and absolutely should, turn off the self-evaluation spigot.

And that place is the place where you indulge your inner child by doing all of the artistic things that child has been waiting to do ever since he or she finally gave up, and accepted as true that art just isn't worth doing unless you're really *good* at it.

"Good" is the enemy of doing art. And doing art is the friend of your inner child.

And you, finally, as a person in midlife, get to be friends again with your inner child.

So, clearly, it's the whole *idea* of "good" that's got to go.

Not that your inner child—not that the *real* you—ever gave a spoon of beans about "good" or "best" or "good enough" anyway.

Nah.

All your inner child ever wanted to do was the *one* thing few adults ever do, which is to have real and honest fun.

Go buy some paints, some brushes, and some paper.

Get a drum.

Take a dance class.

Write a ton of poetry—and give yourself permission not to "edit" a single word of it as you let it pour out of you.

Buy some clay. Throw it on a table, put a bowl of water next to you for dipping your hands into, and dig in.

Have some fun.

Express yourself.

Do art—but only the kind a capital "A."

You know: The kind you were born to do.

CHAPTER 6: HEALTH

Next box up? The one with the gift tag reading *Health*.

And when you lift the lid off that box, what do you find?

A bicycle wheel.

Have you ever held a really good, ready-to-go bicycle wheel on either side, by its hub ends, and then had someone give it a spin? The minute that thing starts going, it's like holding on to magic. The wheel glides so effortlessly, spins so silkily. It's big, but so delicate and light. And it feels like it can go round and round forever—like that's exactly what it *wants* to do.

There's just something satisfyingly harmonious about a spinning, perfectly balanced bicycle wheel.

And they come in such big boxes, too!

"I HATE GRAVITY."

In an extremely informal survey, I asked a good number of my friends and associates what they liked least about being middle-aged.

I am going to guess that you can guess how they most often responded to that question. And if you're middle-aged, then I *know* that you know how they most often responded to it. Because it would very likely be the first way that you would answer that question, too.

"What I like least about being middle-aged," said one friend, capturing the sentiment of all, "is what it's done to my body."

Or, as one of my other friends put it, "The thing I dislike the most about middle-age is how much it makes me hate gravity."

Hearing those words immediately reminded me of a time when, five or six years earlier, I was at the apartment of my friend Nikki. It was a late summer afternoon, and the two of us were visiting over a glass of wine before we headed out to a concert.

We were talking about all the crazy things women do in order to make themselves appear more beautiful, when Nikki groaned, and said, "You've done the mirror test, right?"

"Mirror test?" I said.

She looked at me as if I'd just declared that I'd never in my life heard of the moon. "Yeah. The mirror test." When she could see that I had not become enlightened on the matter in the previous five seconds, Nikki summarily turned away and walked out of the room. In a moment she was back, carrying a large hand-held mirror.

She set the mirror on the table before me. "There. Look into that."

I picked up the mirror and looked into it.

"No, no," she said. "Leave the mirror flat on the table. Stand up, and then bend forward, until your face is directly above the mirror."

"But why?" I said.

"Just do it," said Nikki. "And prepared to be horrified."

Puzzled, I stood, bent, and brought my face over the mirror.

And while I can't say that I was exactly horrified at what I saw, I can't quite say that I wasn't, either.

"Oh my gosh!" I said, looking back up at Nikki.

"Right?" she said. "Can you believe all the flesh, just *hanging* off your face everywhere? I can tell you, that didn't happen to my face when I was a teenager. You know what that is? You know what you're seeing when you look in a mirror that way?"

"What?" I said.

"Gravity! You're looking at evil, terrible, beauty-ravaging *gravity!*"

"Oh," I said. "Then it's official. I hate gravity."

"I'll drink to that," she said.

YOU ARE THE CHANGE

As you know by now, I am an unbridled fan of midlife. I feel that way because I know that midlife is the prime time of life. If you're in midlife, then everything about your life is poised to get better—and probably even radically better—than it's ever been before.

Everything. Better.

Everything, that is, except for the very slight exception of just one, single, itsy-bitsy, tiny little thing.

And that thing is your body.

Sad to say, your body does not get better in middle-age.

Let's face it: It gets worse.

Your body starts hurting more; it starts aching in all kind of places it never did before; tendons and muscles that used to bend and flex like they were made of elastic now feel like they're made of rusty iron; if you hang your face over a mirror it's all you can do not to scream.

If you're middle-aged, I don't have to say anything more about any of this, because I know that you know what I'm talking about.

And if you haven't yet reached middle-aged, then trust me: You have no idea.

All that said, let me say this: If I could wave my magic wand, and nobody's body would ever get one iota worse during middle-age (and so probably during old age, too—though I suppose these are the kinds of details I would have to work out with the magic genie granting me this amazing wish), I wouldn't.

I wouldn't change a single thing. All the creaks and groans and aches and pains that come with middle-age: I'd keep them all.

Why?

Because change is hard. It's *so* hard. What we do, and how we feel, and how we respond to the world, and what we think of our-selves—all of that is so deeply engrained within ourselves that we need something really dramatic to happen if we're going to shake ourselves out of those old notions of who we are, and change into something better.

Wishing that our bodies didn't change in midlife is like wishing that a snake could never shed its skin. If a snake could never shed its skin, then it could never grow.

And, sure, maybe that's not the best example to use. Maybe you're okay with snakes never becoming bigger snakes. If so, then look at it this way: if tarantula spiders could never molt, then ...

So, if crabs never outgrew their exoskeleton ...

Ew.

Well, anyway, the point is that we all need to grow.

And for all of the reasons that we've talked about thus far—the changing realities of our current lives; how unlikely it is that the emotional and psychological mechanisms and paradigms which allowed us to survive and even thrive in our lives before middle-age will continue to serve us well during midlife and beyond; the massive amount of knowledge, experience and wisdom that we've accumulated in our lives, which in and of itself necessitates our reconfiguring into a more expansive and comprehensive understanding not just the totality of who we are, but of whom, at this point in our lives, we can feel more than safe allowing ourselves to be and become—we *must* grow during midlife.

So I am grateful for the changes that occur in our bodies during midlife. Because you can argue about a lot of things. And there are a lot of things the essential properties of which are open to all kinds of differing ideas and interpretations.

But you know what nobody in the whole wide world can argue about?

Gravity.

Old age.

What comes to all of us when our old age is over.

SWING TIME

In midlife, we have no choice. We *will* change. Our bodies *will* become a whole lot different than the only bodies we've ever known before.

That game will get played. And once your personal edition of the Your New Midlife Body game is underway, your choice of responses will fairly quickly boil down to exactly two. You can either join the game, and do all you can to ensure that it goes the way you'd most like it to go; or you can park yourself on the sidelines of the game, refuse to participate in it, and hope for the best.

I think you can guess which of those two options I would heartily encourage you to choose.

But first, let's look at someone who chose the other one—for awhile, at least.

All of his life—literally, from the time he could barely toddle about—Peter had been an athlete. And it was no surprise that he was, for his father had been a professional football player in Germany.

And Peter's father, a strict and even severe disciplinarian, had never left an option in Peter's life other than that he, too, become not just a good athlete, but a great athlete. Peter's entire childhood was spent, every night and during most weekends, with his father playing football. His dad had a whole catalog of training drills, and he made sure to put Peter through each and every one of them, over and over again.

"He would stand me in front of the goal in the field near our house, and kick endless balls at me," Peter told me. "And if I missed one—if I let him score on me—then I'd have to do a bunch of push-ups, or run twice around the field, or whatever other punishment he came up with. But mostly he would just look so disgusted at me, for what an obvious failure as a goalie I was, that more than anything else that would motivate me to try even harder to stop his next kick. And all the kicks after that."

By the time Peter was in high school, he's won so many athletic ribbons and trophies that it was clear he was going to become a major football player, just like his father had been. His coaches were impressed, and even a little intimidated, by the ferocity with which Peter competed.

"Oh, I was a maniac," Peter said. "I didn't let up, ever. I didn't know how. I didn't even know how to play a fun little neighborhood game with the guys. I mean, I did—that's all any of my friends and I ever did, was play football. We were all athletes. I just played the game a lot harder than anyone else did. I'd get the ball, and just … go. Sometimes I'd end a play, or whatever, and look up, and see one of my friends looking at me like I was crazy. In fact, they used to call me "Wolf"—as in "Peter and the Wolf." They said I played like I was some kind of scary wolf."

Without getting into the details of his whole career, Peter had essentially just made his splash in the world of top-tier professional soccer when he suffered a catastrophic knee injury from which he never fully recovered.

Five years after his injury, his athletic career was over. The kid everyone thought would zoom to the top was proven mortal, after all.

"Once I knew I was done with soccer, everything ended for me," Peter told me. "I just didn't know who I was anymore. I just spiraled downward. It got really bad. I was lucky, though, in that I got a job selling athletic equipment and training materials, so at least I had that. But that put me on the road a lot. So I was always in hotels, drinking and smoking, taking my customers out to lavish dinners and so on. And it just wasn't good. Here," he said, handing me a picture he'd taken from his wallet. "This is what I looked like five years ago."

The man I saw in the picture he handed me was not someone I think anyone would ever guess had once been an athlete. Unlike the man sitting across from me in my office, the man in the picture had a huge beer belly. He was holding half a fat cigar in one hand, and a beer in the other. He didn't look too happy.

"I keep that picture with me to remind me of where I was," he said. "Those were bad times. They could have been worse; I could have had no job. I just didn't know what to do with myself. I could feel myself—I could see myself! —getting more and more overweight, and less and less active. You can see how much I weighed, what kind of shape I was in. And it got worse than you see in this picture.

"Finally, when I was around forty-five or six, I kind of thought

I was going to die—or at least have a heart attack or something. I smoked, I drank, and I ate nothing but red meat. And it finally all started to take a real toll on my body.

"Finally, my wife begged me to go the doctor. At first I was, like, "Nah; I know my body better than any doctor could. I know what I need. I'll handle this." But the truth was, I was afraid to see a doctor. I didn't want to know what I was pretty sure he was going to tell me. So I kept putting it off. But then one day my wife got so upset by my lousy condition that she started crying about it. Really crying. When I saw how much pain I was causing to the woman I love so much, I told her that I'd go."

What Peter was told by his doctor was pretty much everything he'd been afraid he might. Peter had high blood pressure; his cholesterol numbers were alarmingly bad; his liver was producing too much fat.

In short, the news wasn't good.

"But I didn't know what to *do* about it," he told me. "I knew I had to change my diet, and quit smoking and drinking so much. But the idea of exercising—which of course I knew I also needed to start doing—just seemed so foreign to me, in a way. I only knew how to do hardcore sports. I couldn't imagine myself working out in a gym, or riding a stationary bicycle, or any of that stuff, without any real purpose to it—without it being so that I could play better."

Peter looked quite sad. "I'd just lost touch with my body, is all it was. I felt like my body had betrayed me so much, and so thoroughly, that I didn't want to get back into any kind of relationship with it, basically." Then he shrugged. "And you saw where that got me," he said. "Because it's also not like I knew anything about moderation. And especially not physical moderation.

"I only ever had one speed. And that was tenth gear. So the whole idea of eating moderately—much less working out moderately—was so alien to who I was that it was like the doctor had told me to start speaking only Mandarin. That just wasn't something I knew how to do."

And then one night something changed in Peter's life. It started with his wife, Diane.

"One Saturday night she just *told* me that we were going out. She laid out on our bed the clothes she wanted me to wear—it was just slacks and a nice shirt—and said, "Put those on. We're going out."

""Where?"" I said. She told me that it was a surprise. I don't tend to like surprises, so I told her I wasn't going anywhere until she told me where it was. But then she gave me a look that twenty years of being married to her told me I shouldn't waste my time trying to fight against. So I got dressed, and off we went."

And where was Diane taking her husband?

"It was the coolest place," said Peter. "It was like an old-fashioned nightclub—the kind with a stage for the band, and a big dance floor, and all these booths set around the floor, where you could sit and drink and watch people dance. But the main thing was that it turned out to a place where they play swing music. That's my very favorite kind of music. Benny Goodman, Tommy Dorsey—I love all that stuff. And, of course, Diane knows that."

As they sat at their table, right off the dance floor, enjoying the live music and the food, Diane put no pressure whatsoever on Peter. Outside of she herself not ordering anything to drink stronger than seltzer water, she didn't try to influence what Peter ordered, either from the bar or the restaurant.

All she wanted him to do was hear the music, see the dancers, and enjoy the moment.

With the intuition of a woman who knows her husband as well as she knows herself, Diane suspected, or at the very least hoped, that if Peter only heard the music he loved so much being played live, he might—he just *might*—be moved to dance a little himself.

Just a little. But that little bit of dancing, she knew, might prove enough.

And sure enough, it did. At some point in the evening, Diane gave Peter a little look, and the next thing he knew, he was up with her on the dance floor.

"Oh, I'm a terrible dancer," said Peter, remembering the night. "On a football field, I was as graceful as Baryshnikov. But on a dance floor?" He laughed. "I'm like Baryshnikov wearing cement shoes. But, you know what? I loved the music so much that night, that I didn't care how I looked. I didn't care if I was any good. I was just having fun. It was *fun* to dance with Diane. Really fun. More fun than I'd had … I don't know. Maybe ever.

"As we were driving home that night, I was telling Diane what a great time I'd just had with her. She suggested that we take one of the swing dance classes they teach at the club. I didn't say much about it—I didn't think much about it—until the following Saturday night, when I saw that Diane had, yet again, laid out an outfit for me.

"But this time, of course, I knew where we were going. And I said okay.

"And I had as much fun that night as I'd had the week before.

"And that's when I started to think, you know, this might be a real thing. This might be something I could do. Something I could actually get into."

Peter started to talk to me from a place deeper within himself than he had been. "So we started taking these dance classes together," he said. "And the thing I started to realize—like, during our very first class—was that I hadn't enjoyed moving, or using, my body, in so long, that I kind of started to wonder if I ever really had. Back when I was doing sports—which meant my whole life before suddenly I wasn't doing sports anymore—my body had really ever only been more of a tool than anything else: something that I just trained and used for a very specific purpose, you know?

"But as we were taking these dance classes, I kind of started to realize that I didn't really enjoy football all that much. I mean, I did: I loved it, really. But in another way, what I really loved *most* about it was the winning part. The part where I scored the goals. Where I was the star. Where I'm the guy who made sure we won the matches."

Peter paused now, and took a while to finish his thought.

"Where I played well enough for even my dad to be happy," he said. In a near whisper, he added, "Not that that happened very often." For a moment Peter seemed lost in his thoughts.

"Anyway," he continued, "It was while taking these dance classes with Diane that I realized that moving my body—especially along with that music I like so much—was just *fun*. I'd never really just had fun moving my body around before. But here I was, doing it. And it didn't have anything to do with winning, or pushing myself as far as I possibly could, or keeping to a training schedule, or anything. It wasn't about anything but just enjoying yourself.

"I know it sounds stupid, but it was like I had rediscovered ... I don't know, something I'd never even known before. And it kind of changed everything for me. I'd never thought of myself as a dancer. But, it turns out, I am! Or, at least, I'm a guy who has a great time dancing with his wife. And, it turns out, that was enough for me. That was more than enough. I love it. And I've lost a ton of weight swing dancing with my wife. My cholesterol's down, my blood panel is all good; I stopped drinking ... and all of it's just because one night Diane took me to a club.

"You know, she's has always acted like her taking me out that first night was nothing; that she hadn't thought anything about how we might start taking dance lessons together. But you know what?" Peter smiled. "I think that girl knew exactly what she was doing."

I wanted to share Peter's story with you because I think it well illustrates three key truths about midlife:

1. As in midlife your body changes, so must you. The great thing about midlife is also the awful thing about midlife: it forces upon you a hierarchy of needs that is brand new in your life, and that you cannot do a single thing to change.

Once you're in middle-age, the condition of your physical health insinuates itself right up at the top of your life concerns—whether you want it to or not. Something to which you may have given little to no thought of in the past now becomes something that it's not possible for you to ignore—or at least not at your peril.

This is not to say that in midlife you can't be in the absolute best shape of your life: you certainly can be. But it is to say that, for likely the first time of your life, you're going to have to proactively, intentionally, and with some assiduousness tend to the maintenance of that good health. The good old days, when you can just take your good health for granted, are over.

Staying healthy throughout midlife will or won't be challenging for you, depending upon how well you've taken care of your health in the past. If you already have good eating and exercising habits, then you're not going to have the kind of trouble in midlife that our friend Peter had.

But if you do find yourself as Peter did—then you can change, the way Peter did.

Midlife—its actual, unavoidable, inevitable power—turned Peter into someone he'd never thought of himself as being.

It turned him—a tough, cigar-chomping, ferocious competitor —into a dancer.

That is the magic of midlife: It invites you to become a newer and happier version of yourself. It teaches you a better way. It reveals to you what you need to do in order to shed from your life everything that's keeping your life from feeling like a wonderful thing you really want to participate in every single day.

Midlife isn't the beginning of the end. It is—or can be, if we only let it be—the start of something wonderfully new.

2. Use your midlife to break with the worst of your earlier life. As we've discussed before, midlife is a time for breaking away from everything in your life that's holding you back from feeling as whole and fulfilled as you know you'd like to, and could, feel.

The miracle of midlife is that it uses your body to empower you to do that. It essentially forces the issue. If you continue to live into your middle-age with the same tired, limited, toxic ideas about yourself and the world that you've been carrying around inside of you for so long, then you'll be unhappier about your life than you've ever been before. Because now, what has always been to you primarily psychological burdens starts to manifest in your body as physical burdens, too.

Peter didn't grow greatly overweight, and develop dangerously high blood-pressure, because he took such awful care of himself. He took such awful care of himself because his father taught him that he was only as lovable as he was successful as an athlete.

But Peter's body knew better. His core self knew better. His higher, warmer, kinder nature knew better.

And all his feet had to do was catch on. Once they had—once Peter was out on the dance floor, forgetting all about what his body was supposed to be doing, and just letting it do what it crazily enjoyed doing—Peter started living a whole new life. A happy life. A real life.

A life on his terms, and nobody else's. Not even his dad's.

That's the freedom and joy awaiting anyone in midlife who has reason to believe that their body is trying to tell them something that their mind and spirit should really, finally, start hearing.

3. Do what your body is telling you it wants to do. Too often we are told in midlife what kind of workout we should do, what kinds of foods we must eat, what sort of regimes we must adhere to.

But where is the fun in that?

And if your life doesn't get more fun the more you do it, then … then I say you're not doing it right.

I don't know about you, but I didn't come through all the life I have so far in order to start getting grim about my life. I want to enjoy my life, not simply endure it.

I want to have fun. And so, I am sure, do you.

Well, anyone in midlife can start having the very best kind of fun the very moment they listen to that good old, life-long companion of theirs, their body.

If you listen to your body, it will tell you what it wants to do in order to feel good and be happy. At any and every moment, your body is trying to communicate to you all of the information you need about what you should do to maximize how your body feels in the real physical world.

I'm not saying you don't need to go to the doctor for your annual check-ups, and all that sort of thing. Of course you do: modern medicine is phenomenal, and only a fool fails to take as much advantage of it if they can. What I *am* saying is that you know what physical activities you most enjoy doing.

If, when you were a kid, you spent as much time on your bicycle as you did on your feet, go out today and buy yourself a bicycle! If as a kid you were pretty sure that you were supposed to have been born a fish, then find the nearest pool or body of water, and jump in! Become the fish you were supposed to be!

And if you don't know what you might be happiest doing physically—what "exercise" to you wouldn't feel like exercising at all —be like Peter. Just start listening.

And if you're literally listening—to music, that is—and you find yourself tapping your foot, then you never know. You might have a be-boppin' swinger in you yet, just dying to get out.

And remember this, always: It doesn't matter what kind of shape you're in right now. If you're still alive, you can get healthy.

It's all a matter of doing what you don't have any choice about anyway, which is starting exactly where you're at.

ONE STEP AT TIME

The thing about midlife is that its effects happen very slowly. No one wakes up morning, and goes, "Oh. Now I'm fat and stiff." They gain weight ounce by ounce, pound by pound, over the course of many, many years. Little by little, they grow stiffer and stiffer.

It's like rust on a car. One day you see a tiny pinpoint of rust by one of your tire wells, and you basically ignore it. Twenty years later, you slam shut the driver's side door of that same car, and the entire automobile collapses into a heap of rusty metal.

It's not that you hadn't seen all along that the car was growing rustier. It's that it kept holding itself together. It kept working; it kept getting you from one place to the other. That was good enough.

Until suddenly it wasn't, of course.

The real problem with our bodies in middle-age isn't usually that they fall apart all of a sudden—although certainly none of us want to take lightly even the possibility of our, or of anyone we know and love, having, say, a heart attack. You recall our story about Christine, and the heart attack her husband suffered. I told that story in the context of Christine discovering that she did, in fact, have the confidence that it took her to take over her husband's business—but of course the deeper story there was how traumatized she and her children—and certainly not less so her husband—were by that heart attack.

Heart attacks are terrible. Let's all agree never to have one, shall we? And let's further agree that there is a whole lot of things we can do to ensure that we never do have one.

Let's agree that there is never any reason for us to throw up our hands and declare that there's really nothing we *can* do to reverse whatever less-than-optimal physical condition we might happen to find ourselves in once we're in our midlife years.

Because there is *always* something that we can do to improve our well-being, no matter how small that thing is. And when it comes to regaining the physical health that is, in fact, our very birthright—a natural and wonderful thing, to which everyone is entitled—a little almost invariably becomes a lot.

I'd like you to know my friend Marta. Not too long ago, Marta was unhappy. Hers wasn't the kind of unhappiness that might have resulted from a specific sad or unfortunate thing happening to her or to someone she loves, though. It was more ... well, I'll let her tell you herself. All of the words between now and the end of this chapter are Marta's:

When I was young I was athletic. I loved swimming, bicycling, hiking, skiing—just about anything that combined being active with being outdoors.

Twenty-five years of marriage and three children later, however, and I wasn't that person anymore.

And, honestly, sometimes—and much too often, that's for sure—I didn't know who I was.

The one thing I did know about the person I had become, though, was that I did not enjoy being that person.

That person was always tired. She was always feeling down. She never had any energy; or never any extra energy, anyway—which is the kind of energy that it takes to have fun.

And there was no denying it: She was fat. Really fat. The kind of fat that comes from way, way too long spent sitting around an empty-nest house watching television and eating cake and cookies and chocolate and potato chips and you name it.

It was just a terrible time of life for me. My husband and I lived together more as brother and sister who don't much care for each than we did as husband and wife. The big activity of my day was going back to bed the second my husband left home to go to his office.

I knew I had to change; if nothing else (and this was hardly nothing), my chest was starting to hurt whenever I did anything even slightly physically taxing. I was, I knew, a heart attack waiting to happen.

But I couldn't shake the inertia that was weighing down everything that my life had become; in the end, every single day, my fear of having that heart attack lost to my inability to gather the muster to do anything to stave it off.

And then one day something really interesting happened. I was in my usual prone position on the couch, staring dead-eyed at a television show, when the time came for me to change the channel so that I could watch the show I always watched at that time.

But there was a problem. I couldn't find the remote control.

Or, rather, I *could* have found the remote control, since I knew it had only slipped off my stomach and now laid buried somewhere near beneath me.

But locating the thing would have entailed my moving. I'd either have to roll first one way on the couch, and then the other, trying to reach my hand beneath myself each time before I rolled back to the middle and likely crushed my hand—or, heaven forbid, I'd have to rouse myself enough to stand up off the couch, and find it that way.

Neither option appealed to me. So, reasoning that the soap opera that was about to start playing probably, after all, wasn't all that boring, I stayed right where I was.

I was maybe ten minutes into watching the soap opera when I knew, beyond a doubt, that it was even more boring than I'd ever thought it might be.

And so my mind started wandering a little bit. Not *too* far, since any kind of wandering constitutes exercise, but it wandered far enough for me to start thinking about—or to at least sharply cognizant of—exactly how lazy I'd become.

Here I was, preferring to stay prone on the couch and be bored to death, rather than simply get up just long enough to find the remote control that was lying somewhere beneath me.

And the thought that I had was, "I have no will power. None. I couldn't move right now if the house were on fire."

Then I pictured the walls around me actually being on fire.

Okay, I thought: Under those circumstances, I'd move. I'd probably wait until my hair was being singed before doing so, but I'd move.

But under normal circumstances?

No. I had no will.

None.

Zero.

My eyes fell upon the bowl of kettle corn sitting near me on the coffee table.

I could, I thought, easily reach out and move that bowl. I could push it a couple of inches on the table.

Unless I truly had no will power, in which case I wouldn't be able to accomplish even that.

So *did* I have any will power, I wondered. Or didn't I?

I reached out, and pushed the bowl just a few inches away from me.

There. I'd done something. I'd proven that I had will power. I'd put my mind to accomplishing a goal, and had indeed accomplished that goal.

This left me rather intrigued. It got me to thinking that it doesn't really matter how small—how really, really small—any goal is that you set for yourself, as long as you achieve that goal. In fact, I reasoned further, the smaller the goal that you set for yourself, the better, because the more assured your success would be at achieving that goal.

I had just willed myself to use my arm and my hand to move that bowl of popcorn.

I wondered if I could bend one of my legs.

Turns out I could. And having my right foot by my left knee felt nice on my back, too.

I started thinking about whether or not I might be able to will myself to get up, get dressed, and go out for a walk.

I immediately knew that there was no way on earth I had that much will power.

Which brought me back to thinking, "Well, how much will power *do* I have?" I had, after all, just willed myself to move a bowl and bend my leg. So clearly I had *some.*

I wondered if I had enough to try and remember where my walking shoes were.

Turn out I did. They were, I recalled, on the floor of my closet next to the dirty clothes hamper.

That little mental exercise completed, I wondered if I had enough will power to stick both my arms straight out in the air, like Dracula about to sit up in his coffin.

As it happened, I did.

Then—what the heck—I wondered if I had enough will power *just* to sit up on the couch.

No more that that, at all, I told myself. Sitting up only. Did I have what it took to do *just* that?

The answer, to my amazement, was yes.

Did I have enough will power, I next asked myself, to stand up? Not to go anywhere, or do anything, or accomplish anything whatsoever—but only to stand up?

Turns out I did.

And I kept testing myself that way, like I was some kind of mouse in a wildly speculative science experiment being conducted by, well, me. And the test kept consisting of the exact same question: Could I will myself to do something—something really small and easy—if I completely disconnected from doing that single thing doing any *other* thing that might naturally be connected to, or flow from, that thing?

Could I *only* sit up—and nothing else? Yes.

Could I *only* stand up—and nothing else? Yes.

Could I *only* walk first into my bedroom—and then into my closet?

Yes and yes.

In this way—but taking just these little, isolated, mini baby steps—did I find myself, finally, dressed in my best sweats, and taking a walk outside.

And I went through that same process the next day. I never once willed myself to take a walk; that would have been more than I wanted to handle. But I could tell myself to *only* do this one thing —and then, once that was done, decide to do *only* do one other thing; and so on, and so on, until, once more, I found myself taking a walk.

That was about a year ago. Today, I have lost fifty pounds, I've learned to cook healthier (and tastier!) foods than I've ever eaten before, and I'm just a much, much happier person than I was back when I was lying motionless on the couch helplessly watching a boring soap opera.

Today, I am still convinced that the best way to make a real and lasting change in your life isn't to set a big goal for yourself, and to then hope you have the will power to achieve that goal. It is, rather, to break down even the largest goal into such small individual goals that you can't help but accomplish those.

You know that saying about how a journey of a thousand miles begins with a single step? Well, I say that even that single step can be a bit much. It was for me, anyway. If it is for you, too, then I think it's best to forget all about that first step. Just put it right on out of your mind.

But could you do a half-step? Could you just *lean* forward a little bit?

Could you do *nothing* but put on first one sock and shoe, and then the other sock and shoe?

Could you do *nothing* but stand outside?

Nothing but take one single step?

Nothing but walk to the end of your driveway?

Nothing but walk to the end of your street?

Let the thousand miles take care of itself.

And I'd like to say one more thing.

When I was in the worst of the shape I got in, it was unimaginable to me that I could ever think that my middle-aged body was, or ever could be, beautiful. One of the things that I think kept me on the couch eating my heart out was the conviction I had that, even if I lost all the weight, and became as beautiful as I could be, I'd still only be half as beautiful as I had been when I was, say, twenty years old.

No matter what, I knew, I'd still be middle-aged. Things that weren't supposed to bulge would probably still bulge. I'd still sag and droop in places where, I believed, sagging and drooping were not supposed to occur.

But you know what happened? The better shape I got in—and, again, without really trying to get in any better shape at all—the more I came to find that I loved my body.

I felt that I had—by having and raising my children, by being a good and faithful wife, just by living for as long as I had—earned every single one of my wrinkles and sags and flabs.

The more I thought about it, the more I realized that, contrary to what I thought I thought, I *didn't,* in fact, want the body of a twenty-year-old anymore. Because that body would not at all reflect the truths that I had spent my whole life learning. I came to feel that all of my non-teenage body "flaws" were like medals that military generals are always showing off on their uniform jackets.

And then I started wondering who in the world just *decided* that the only kind of body worth having—or at least the *best* kind of body to have—was one that nobody who'd had any significant life experience at all could possibly have?

We love old homes, old paintings, old trees.

So what's our problem with older bodies?

And the more I started looking around at both women and men, the more I started seeing that older bodies aren't any less beautiful than younger bodies. They're just *different.*

What older bodies have that younger bodies *don't* have is evidence of life.

And what could be more beautiful, more valuable, than that?

CHAPTER 7: BETTER RELATIONSHIPS

Two boxes left!

On the tag of the one you approach next, you read the words *Better Relationships.*

You lift the lid, and see that inside the box are two lovely hand-crafted teacups (with their saucers, of course), along with a jar of loose-leaf oolong tea.

Why oolong? Because it's fun to say, and it's one of my very favorite kinds of tea.

Why tea at all? Because sharing a cup of tea with someone isn't like texting, instant messaging, phoning, Face-timing, Skyping, Tweeting, Snapchatting, Instagramming, or emailing them.

When you share of cup of tea with someone, you must really *be* there with them.

When you drink a cup of tea with someone, something real and present is necessarily happening between you and that person. Something *transactional* is going on between the two of you.

It may not be a great transaction. It might not be something wonderful enriching or profoundly meaningful.

But it *will* be something real.

And being real is what middle-age is all about.

All humans are—and are perhaps above all—social creatures. We are all of us designed to function within, belong to, and be nurtured by others.

We must have relationships. And I mean that both from the perspective of our natural desires—we all want and need to be in relationship with others—and literally, as a matter of simple fact: from the very moment we are born, we are already in at least one of the most important relationships of our lives.

We arrive in relationship with others; we spend our lives in relationship with others; we pass from this life in relationship with others.

A life lived in too much seclusion is a tragedy. It's the opposite of just about everything that human beings are designed to do. That is why when the keepers of prisons want to maximally punish an inmate, they put them in solitary confinement. They do this because they know that one of the worst things you can do to a person is to remove them from the possibility of any contact with others.

Again: We must have our relationships.

So integral are our relationships to our understanding and experience of everything that we are, feel, hope for, and know, that I think it's fair to say that no single factor determines the quality of our lives as does the quality of the relationships in our lives.

And what most determines the quality of the relationships in our lives?

But of course: The quality of the relationship we have with ourselves.

So we see the continuous loop, the Mobius strip-like phenomenon, in which we all exist: It is largely (and some might reasonably argue exclusively) the quality of the first and most important relationships in our lives (and I'm looking at you, every mother and father) which then determines the quality of the relationship we have with ourselves, which then determines the quality of the relationships we have with others.

And in this way can so much of our lives feel to us like we're stuck in some kind of bizarro, ever-evolving hall of mirrors.

Everywhere we look, there we are, reflected back to ourselves. Sometimes the reflection is a little distorted, sometimes a lot; sometimes it's twisted or warped, sometimes it's not. But always, essentially, it is us, looking back at us.

Thus does a woman marry a man either just like or radically opposite her father; thus does a man (to quote the title of the iconic American song) want a girl just like the girl who married dear old dad.

That tends to be the pattern of our lives. We do what we know. We behave as we've learned to behave. We look for relationships —all kinds of relationships—that feel to us like the relationships which formed the very person we are.

If you were raised in a psychologically healthy environment, then for you this is a largely good and positive phenomenon, for there is no place so warm as home.

If, however, you were raised in psychologically unhealthy or dysfunctional environment, this repeating dynamic tends to play out in a much more problematic way. For it is not just the criminal who tends to return to the scene of the crime: it is, alas, also the victim.

For better or worse, this cycle of been there, done that, doing that again is the one around which most of us continue to go around.

With the great gift(s) of midlife, however, we can break that cycle. Midlife is *meant* to break that cycle.

All of our lives, we have been one person—the person we were essentially created to be: the person we were formed as, the person we became in response to the shaping of those in control of our most formative years, the only person we've ever known how to be.

And then we enter middle-age.

And that is when, for the very first time, we've finally been on this earth long enough to have amassed, first-hand, a body of knowledge and experience so vast that, if we but let it, can guide us on a journey towards discovering who we were way back before everybody around us started telling us whom they wanted (and needed) us to be.

Finally, in midlife, we get to say who we are—and what we want, and what we need, and why we want and need whatever we know we want and need.

Finally, we get to tell ourselves who we are, because we know that no one else could possibly do that for us—or not, at any rate, do it and get it right.

Finally, we get the relationship with ourselves that we've always wanted.

And guess what? Anyone who wants to continue being in relationship with us has to get on board with the new person we've become.

And if they don't?

Then we're okay with that, too.

Because we're middle-aged. And that means we know who we are.

MERRY CHRISTMAS, LILY

For twelve years, a client of mine (whom I'll call Lily) was an art teacher at a community college. A few years back, right at the beginning of a new school year, she and a number of her fellow teachers were laid off from the school, due to budget reductions.

This was, of course, a shocking and depressing turn of events for Lily. But her husband owned a successful business, so she was at least able to afford staying home for a while—or permanently, if she so desired—so that she could deal with the new reality of her life. This was in September.

That Christmas, Ian, Lily's husband of over twenty years, left her.

He chose Christmas morning (and yes, you read that correctly: Christmas morning) to inform Lily that he was so in love with a girl he'd hired at his company maybe eight months before, and with whom he'd been having an affair for the previous six months, that he and the girl (who was—surprise! —half his age) had decided to live together, starting on that very day.

Within a half-hour of Ian informing her of his whole new plan for his whole new life, Lily found herself all alone in the big house in which she and her husband had raised their two children—the youngest of whom had, not a week before she'd been let go from her job, followed her older brother off to college.

That Christmas was not a merry one for Lily.

"Just like that, everything was gone," she told me. "Everything. It was like the whole slate of my life had been simply wiped clean. Except I was still *on* that slate. It's just . . . I was *alone* on it. I was so shocked. I was numb. After Ian walked out the door—which he did after criticizing me for, as he put it, doing nothing since I'd been fired but lie around the house all day feeling sorry for myself—I just sat on the couch. I couldn't move. I didn't call anyone; I didn't go outside; I didn't watch television. I'm not even sure I ate. I just sat there, listening to the deafening roar silence that my life had become."

Lily might not have called anyone; but someone did call her. It was her sister, Sophia, who lived about one thousand miles away, and who called her every Christmas evening.

"I told Sophia what had happened," said Lily, "and she started railing about how much she had always hated Ian, and about how much she'd always known that one day he would leave me. I can't say that it was a conversation that made me feel great—but, in a way, it did, because she was saying things about my husband— about my ex-husband, as I was already having to think of him— that I couldn't even think yet, let alone express."

In the course of their conversation, Sophia invited Lily to come and live with her and her family.

"At first I said no," Lily told me. "The idea wasn't even something I could comprehend. I was in my house. It was the home Ian and I had built. It was where our children lived. Except, that, as I was talking to Sophia—or, rather, listening to her, since I could barely manage to say anything at all—it slowly began to dawn on me that the house I was in had become a tomb. That's how it felt to me, sitting right there on my couch: like a tomb. Everything was gone. My husband was gone. My children didn't live there anymore. Even our dog had died not long before.

"I was alone. I was forty-five years old, and alone. And in a way I was even *worse* than alone, because I knew that my husband had basically traded me in for a younger, prettier model. Somehow knowing he was with someone else made me feel more alone than I think I would have felt otherwise. I don't know. All I know is that, as I was listening to Sophia talk to me about my moving in with her—or at least staying with her and her family until I could start a new life for myself in their city—the more it started to make sense.

"What was in it for me to stay? Nothing but memories—all of which had forgotten me, is how it felt.

"Next thing I know," Lily continued, "I'm telling Sophia that if she's serious about inviting me to come stay with her, I would. She said, "Yes! Do! We'd love to have you! Come! There's a great art scene in this city. You'll love it!"

"The next morning I filled up my car with everything I wanted to take with me, locked the door behind me, and drove off towards my new life. It was a weird experience, looking in my car's rearview mirror, and seeing my whole life growing smaller and smaller as I drove away from it."

I don't wish for anyone to have the experience that Lily did that Christmas morning. Of course not!

But, as much as it hurt her when it happened, Ian's leaving her—and especially in the way that he did: sniping at her on Christmas morning as he marched out the door and slammed it behind him—was the best thing that ever happened to Lily.

DOWN BY THE RIVER

Sophia had been right about her city: it was a veritable Mecca for artists of all sorts, from far and wide.

"The whole art scene there was just thriving," said Lily. "It was —it still is, and had been for at least a decade before I got there —absolutely amazing. I thought I had been living in a place with a great and thriving art scene. And I had been! But it was nothing compared to where Sophia lived. I knew her city had its share of artists and galleries. I just had no idea how many of them there were.

"I also had no idea how *good* they were. This wasn't a city filled with amateur and hobbyist artists. This was a deep and wide community of serious, dedicated, visionary-type artists—people who made a *living* doing their art. These were *real* artists. It was like I'd moved to Paris in the twenties, or something like that. The artistic community—and its variety—was that strong.

As exciting and stimulating as Lily found her new environs to be, she also found it intimidating.

"I'd always thought of myself as an artist," she told me. "And I was. I *taught* art, for one. But even more than teaching others how to do art, I did art myself. I'm a painter. I work in oils. I've always done small, meticulous landscapes. And they're good, too. I've won my share of ribbons at local art shows, and that sort of thing.

"But this, where Sophia lived, was a whole other level of art and artists. The more I looked around the city in which I was now living—the more galleries I went into, the more artists I talked to, the more studios I visited—the less of an artist I felt like."

I encouraged her to tell me more about that feeling of hers.

"Well, what I came to feel," she said, "was that maybe I wasn't really an artist at all—or much of one, anyways. Because I'd been painting what I'd been painting—or different versions of the same painting—for so long that, at that point, I had to admit to myself that I was really more of a craftsperson than I was anything like a genuine artist.

"Not that there's anything wrong with craftspeople," she hastened to add. "All great artists are great craftspeople, and vice versa. (The two are a lot closer than people tend to think.) It was just that, as I came to realize, what I had been making for almost as long as I could remember wasn't really art—insofar as I wasn't doing anything that was at all *new* to me. And in a very true way, if it ain't new, it ain't art.

"What I was doing was playing it safe. I was never allowing myself to be in anything but full control of every stroke of my brush. I always knew exactly what every picture that I started was going to look like when it was finished. And there's nothing necessarily wrong with that. But that's *all* I ever did. And if you're an artist, there *is* something wrong with that.

"And my pictures were *boring.* They really *were* all the same—and what they were wasn't exactly galvanizing. Or challenging. Or *anything.* Just about *all* they were was executed well. I was mistaking technical proficiency for artistic vision. But those two aren't the same thing at all. And when I realized they weren't—when I realized I'd been mistaking the one for the other—I kind of collapsed inside."

I asked her to talk to me about what she meant by that.

"I mean I just … fell apart," she said. "First I'd been a mother—and then I wasn't, because my children were adults. Then I'd been a wife—and then I wasn't, because my husband left me. But the one thing I knew I still was—the *one* thing I'd always been, and knew I'd always be, because nobody could ever take that away from me—was an artist.

"And then … there I was. Forced to face the fact that maybe I wasn't that, either. And if I wasn't even an artist, then I had no idea what was left for me to be. And that left me with nothing.

"I remember the day it all hit me. I had just spent a couple of hours wandering in and out of a bunch of art studios that were housed in what used to be a big brick factory building. It was an open-house type of thing: where the public is invited to just walk around inside the building, and pop into whatever studios they care to, and meet the artists. So that's what I'd done.

"And I left the building, feeling kind of … wiped out. I felt like there was just nothing left inside of me. I could see—I had just seen, time and time again, in one studio after another—that I was no more of an artist than I was a professional golfer. I felt like I was some kind of deceiver, like for my whole life I had been living some kind of pathetic lie—except that the one I had been lying to all these years, the one I had been deceiving, was me.

"Right across the small highway from the studio building was a river. I went over by the river, stood on its banks, and watched the water slowly sliding by. I felt so numb.

"And then something in me just … snapped. All at once I became aware, at the deepest possible level of my being, that … I don't quite know how to say this . . . but that I still had time. That my life wasn't over yet. Yes, my children were off on their own now—which of course I never thought of anything but a good thing, but which still *did* leave a pretty good sized hole right in the middle of my life, where they had been for so, so long. And yes, I'd lost my job, my calling, as I'd always thought of it. And yes, my husband was now off enjoying his new life with his new hot girlfriend, as if he'd never been married to me, or been the father of our children, in his life.

"All of those things had happened, yes. And though they all left me feeling as if I had, in some real and important way, died—the fact was, I very suddenly and very *completely* felt, I had *not* died. I was still alive. I was still here.

"And what in a way I mostly realized, all in what felt like one big kind of *punch*, was that I did not have all of the time left in the world that, right up until that actual moment, I'd always somehow believed I *did* have. What I realized was something that I also realized I'd known, somewhere deep inside of myself, for a long, long time, which was that my pretty little landscapes—my precious little cabins nestled into the woods near the adorable little babbling brook—weren't real art. They were greeting card art. They were calendar art. But they weren't *real*. They didn't show how I really felt. They didn't express anything genuine. They didn't show who I really was.

"Except—and this is the part that just about brought me to my knees, right there by that river—my paintings showed exactly who I was.

"They showed that I was someone who either had nothing true and visceral and urgent to say, or who did, but was just too afraid to say it.

"And the truth, I realized right then, was that I had been the former. But I didn't have *time* to be that anymore. Now I was the latter."

THE ART OF LIVING

From her moment by the river on, Lily's life hasn't been the same.

"I started painting in a way I never had before," she told me. "Instead of doing these very careful and fastidiously realistic landscapes and bucolic little pastoral scenes in oils, I started doing these wild, stormy abstracts in acrylics. I started expressing myself, right there on the canvas, with an immediate, visceral urgency I would have never dared to even think about before.

"And—and this is of course important for an artist—I also started being unafraid to show my work. Before, it was almost like I didn't really want anyone to see my work. I felt shy about it. And that was for a couple of reasons, I think. Part of it was that I had grown up learning that good little girls didn't make a point of making a point of how they really felt. It was basically wrong, I had learned, for me to dare to put my needs, and my desire to express myself, ahead of anyone else's—and especially that of a man's. God forbid that I, a mere female, should take up any of the oxygen in the room that a man might want to breath. And it's still largely men who own the art galleries, who decide whose work is and isn't valuable. So I just ... balked at carrying my pictures around to show gallery owners. I was also sure they wouldn't like them. I desperately wanted them to—but was sure they wouldn't. So I saved myself the heartache that I was so sure was inevitable, and never even tried.

"But after I'd been painting in my new way for only about six months, I was fine with showing my work to anyone. I didn't care anymore. Because I liked my work, and that's all that mattered to me. You can't imagine what a relief that is to someone who never really had a way to evaluate their own work, but through the eyes of others.

"Suddenly, I was the judge. I got to say if any given picture worked or not. I got to decide the value and worth of my work. What could be more liberating than that?

"And you know what happened?"

"What?"

"I got accepted by a gallery. A good gallery, too. One of the big ones in our city. I got accepted by a *couple* of galleries. Gallery owners, other artists, and people generally were suddenly liking my work. It's a funny thing. When I wanted people to like my work, no one cared about it. But the moment I stopped caring if anyone but me liked it or not, other people started liking it."

I asked Lily to talk to me a little about what this new way of seeing herself and her work meant relative to the relationships in her life.

After a moment of quiet thought, she said, "Well, honestly—and you'd already guess this, of course—the most important relationship that really changed was my relationship with myself. It's almost like I'd never known myself before this. I mean, I did know myself, of course. And if anything, in a way I knew myself too well. I had been the person I'd been for so long—a wife, a mother, a teacher—that *that* person was the person I knew, rather than the person who was beneath that person—who basically supported that person—that I most *actually* am." She laughed. "That probably doesn't even make sense, does it?"

"It does," I said.

"Oh, good. So that came first. And then I started painting in the new way. But then, combined with those two things, a third thing started happening. I began to realize something that I hadn't anticipated, which was that I was not angry at anybody.

"You'd expect me to be, right? Or I would, anyway. I figured that naturally, along with this new truth that I'd uncovered about who I really was—that I was an *actual* artist, who had *actual* things she wanted to *actually* express through *actual* art—I would get this surge, from deep down inside of me, of a whole bunch of negative emotions, or certainly a lot of anger, at everything and everyone who had stopped me from knowing maybe the most important thing about myself there *is* to know. I kind of assumed I'd be flooded with anger at Ian for leaving me; or at the head of the art department of the college where I'd taught—someone whom for years I'd considered one of my dearest friends—for not hesitating one moment to put my name at the top of the list of those whom the college should let go; or angry with my parents, for teaching me that the only way I could prove my worth—the only way I really *had* any worth—was if I was always smiling, always complacent, always worried about nothing so much as whether I was looking as cute and pretty, and saying as little, as I possibly could.

"But you know what? I wasn't mad at any of those people. I just … wasn't. Instead, what I felt towards them was actually compassion. I felt *understanding* about who they were, and what they had done.

"It wasn't just my children who had left home; they were my husband's children, too. And his business, which had only grown almost since its inception, had started, for the first time ever, to falter a bit. Just before starting his affair, he had gone in for a physical, where he learned that he wasn't, after all, immortal.

"The bottom line was that there were *reasons* Ian did what he did. And it's not to say that his leaving me—especially the way he did—wasn't wrong. It was wrong: it was shallow and selfish, no doubt about it. But … why be *mad* at him for it, was the way I felt. How was my seething about the way he treated me going to make my life—my new life, my freer life! —any better? How would my being angry at Ian help anything? It wouldn't. It couldn't.

"So I let all my anger at him fall away. And I'm really glad I did. Because then we were able to talk about our separation in a way that was actually helpful and good. I was calm whenever I talked to him about who got what, and how we'd divide our assets, and so on.

"I was able to see him as a *person,* rather than as the man who'd destroyed my life, or whatever. And, of course, that made all the difference in our relationship. Instead of it being rancorous and nasty, it was just, to me, business to be dealt with.

"The same with losing my job. The woman who basically had me fired was a friend of mine. But, the truth was, I had become a bit of a star in her department. I had thought of, and initiated, this whole program, where our art department interacted with a bunch of local elementary schools, to the overall purpose of significantly enhancing their art education. And it worked; the program was a huge hit and rapid growing.

"Well, once things in my heart calmed down, because I had learned who I was, I had the clarity to understand that my friend was simply jealous of me. And I knew enough about her sad childhood to know that, in her world, the rise of what amounted to a sibling meant a lot of bad things happening to her.

"So she'd gotten rid of me. And I know that hurt her. I know it brought her a tremendous amount of guilt and angst. And the reason I know that is because a few days after my River Moment I called her, and we talked about it. We discussed it. She felt *terrible.* I shared with her how getting fired from the college turned out to be one of the greatest things that had ever happened to me. We *healed* around what had happened between us.

"Today, I still call her a friend. And I *know* that wouldn't have happened if I hadn't had that moment standing next to the river.

"It's the same way between me and my parents. My relationship with my mom and dad been highly strained—almost to the point of our breaking entirely—for decades. Now it's perfectly great. Why? Because now I don't ask anything of them. I don't expect anything from them. I don't want anything from them. Now I don't feel the need for them to approve of me, or affirm me, or tell me how much they love me.

"Now I can feel grateful to them for everything they did do for me—for giving me a home, for dressing and feeding me, for sending me to good schools, for never hitting me or my sister the way so many of my friends' parents hit them, and on and on and on. And then I can let how I feel about them *stop,* right there, with that simple and true gratitude. And that's enough. They're decent people who did the best they could with what they know. And that's good enough.

"In short, all of my relationships are really good now. My relationship with Sophia is stronger—much stronger—than it's ever been. My relationship with my kids is everything I could want it to be. I have better friends now than I've ever had in my life. When it comes to my personal relationships, my life has never been better, richer, or more rewarding. Honestly, as glad as I am for what my new understanding of who I am has done for me as an artist, I'd trade all the paint, all the brushes, and all the canvases in the world for what's happened with my personal relationships. Learning how to be with others is the real reward of learning how to be with myself."

These words of Lily's are among the most beautiful I've ever heard. "Learning how to be with others is the real reward of learning how to be with yourself." That really does say it all, doesn't it?

Another (and much more prosaic) way of expressing this is to say that it's *all* about honesty. Once we are honest with ourselves, we can start to be honest with others. We can let them know what we want from them, what we expect from them, what they can and can't expect from us.

We can make all of our relationships *real,* in a way that we just can't until we're being perfectly honest with everyone—most certainly not excluding ourselves.

And how do we manage, finally, to be fully and completely honest with ourselves?

By doing nothing more, and nothing less, than knowing, admitting, and accepting who we really are.

And what is the best, if not the *only* time in our lives when we are ready and able to do that?

You guessed it!

CHAPTER 8: PEACE

Guess what's inside the seventh and final gift awaiting you in the great hallway of middle-age?

Nothing. It's empty.

Surprise!

Except then you see that it's not *quite* empty. For on its bottom, facing up at you, is an image.

And that image is the Chinese symbol for yin and yang.

Black and white, light and dark, positivity and negativity, flowing together and around each other in an exquisitely harmonious dance.

It is the most perfect representation of peace that I know of.

And it's the idea of peace, this *reality* of peace, that I would most like you to hold in your mind—in your spirit, in your heart, in your very soul—from now on.

In his classic book, *The Religions of Man,* Huston Smith tells us that the whole of Hinduism's wisdom and teachings boil down to a single affirmation: You can have what you want.

Which certainly sounds like very good news, does it not?

Of course, it does bring front and center the question which all of us would do well, at literally any moment of our lives, to ask ourselves: What is it, exactly, that I want?

And that is the question that I pose to you now.

What do you want, more than you want anything else?

I am going to guess that when you were young, what you wanted most of all was stimulation, pleasure, the next fun thing.

When a little older, you sought romantic love, professional success, social affirmation.

And now? Today?

At the midway point between your birth and your death, what is it that you want most of all?

I would venture to say that it's balance. That it's understanding. That it's harmony.

That it is, as Mr. Smith puts it, *being:* infinite being, infinite knowledge, and infinite bliss.

Which, taken altogether, may be *just* a bit much for our purposes here.

The way I like to think of it is this: If you are middle-aged, then what you want, above all, is peace.

That, I will dare to presume, is your desire, your goal, your hope: inner, personal peace.

So let's talk about that.

A NEW DAY FOR THE MONKEYS

There is a fourteenth-century Chinese parable by Liu-Ji entitled *Rule by Tricks.* It goes as follows.

There was once an old man who ruled over a pack of monkeys that he had trained to do his bidding. Every morning, Monkey Master (for yes, that is what the locals called him) would herd his monkey minions together in his courtyard, and demand that the eldest of them lead all the other monkeys into the nearby mountains. Once the monkeys had gathered all the fruit they could find growing on the bushes and trees in the mountains, they would return to Monkey Master's home, and immediately hand over to him one-tenth of their bounty for the day. Any monkey who refused to surrender one-tenth of their day's gathering would be ruthlessly beaten by the old man.

As you might well imagine, the monkeys were not thrilled with their lives. But between being cowed by their fear of Monkey Master, and the fact that theirs was the only life any of them had ever known, the monkeys never failed to stay quiet and do exactly as they were told.

One day the monkeys were in the mountains, collecting fruit as usual, when one of the younger, smaller monkeys stopped working. "Hey, everyone!" he said, "I've had a thought."

"So have I," said the nearest monkey. "It was that you should get back to work."

"No, seriously," said the little monkey. "I've been thinking about something. Let me ask you all a question. Did the old man plant all these fruit bushes and trees?"

While a few of them responded by scratching their heads in puzzlement, most of the monkeys agreed that no, the old man hadn't planted any of the fruit bushes and trees.

"These all grew here naturally, right?" said the little monkey.

"Right," said the other monkeys.

"So here's my question," said the little monkey. "If these plants don't belong to the old man because they grew here naturally, then why is it okay for him to order us to collect and bring to him all of this fruit? It doesn't even make sense. Who made him *'Monkey Master,' anyway? Why can't we just come here whenever we want to, and do whatever we —".*

But then the little rabble rouser quit talking, because he could see that, almost as soon as they'd heard his words, everyone in his audience had become enlightened and awakened.

"Oh," said the little monkey. "Okay, then. Cool."

At the end of the day all the monkeys returned to the old man's house, where they all surrendered to him ten-percent of their haul, just like nothing had changed.

But that night, after they were sure Monkey Master was fast asleep, the monkeys got busy tearing down the barracks in which they'd for so long been held prisoner.

"Shhh! Keep it down!" the little revolutionary monkey said to one of the bigger monkeys, who was ferociously tearing off a chunk of roof.

"Why?" said the big monkey. "You couldn't wake up that old man if you fired off a cannon in his bedroom."

"Good point," said the little monkey. "Here, let me help you with that."

Once their former confines had been reduced to rubble, the monkeys broke into the locked hut where the old man stored all of his fruit. Taking back every last piece of it, they then headed back up into the mountains they knew so well, never to return.

Not too long thereafter the Monkey Master died of starvation.

The reason I love this story is because I think of the monkeys as representing just about anyone in midlife. They're doing the only thing they've ever known how to do, which is what they've always learned to do, what they've always thought they were supposed to do. They're too afraid, too stuck in their ways, too limited by their habits and routines, to do or think anything new —even though the way they've always thought, and the ways they've always behaved, isn't doing much of anything for them beyond allowing them to simply survive from one day to the next. It's not good for them. It's not healthy for them. It's not productive for them. But they keep doing it anyways, because it's literally the only life they've ever known.

Do what you're supposed to do, don't complain, suffer as you must—and then do the same thing all over again tomorrow. That's their life. They don't question it, because at the most root core of their idea of who they are they do not think they have any choice.

Which is, of course, an awfully bleak way of describing anyone's life. But you see my point: the monkeys, through what amounts to really know will of their own, just keep doing what it is they've always done—just stay on the course that was set for them before they had any say in their own course at all—despite what, as adults, they are now more than capable of understanding what that course is costing them relative to the quality of their everyday lives.

Until, one day, somebody presents to them the most obvious thought in the world—being that, in actuality, they are free—and in the instant of their hearing it everything for them radically and permanently changes.

Suddenly they *are* free.

Suddenly they get to write the rules for their lives.

Suddenly they're not enslaved by the only past they've ever known.

I always think of those monkeys, the day after their awakening, lazing about on the ground and in the branches of their mountain trees, their bellies swollen with all the fruit they've been rapturously enjoying, sighing contentedly, and saying "Ahh. Now *this* is living. Who knew life could be so easy?"

And I love that, once they stop giving their lives to the service of Mr. Monkey Master, the old man summarily dies. I think it neatly illustrates how true it is that once we finally step out of the exhausted dysfunctional paradigms which have always held us captive, those paradigms simply disappear.

Turns out the door to our prison call has been open all along. All we had to do was push on it.

We go out into the world, every single day of our lives, and work and strive and sacrifice all that we do, and all that we do and all that we are is informed by the unconscious assumption that we are absolutely beholden to, and captured by, all of the rules and regulations set forth for us, at the very beginning of our lives, by what amounts to our own Monkey Master: our parents, the household in which we grew up, the culture which everywhere and constantly tells us, in a million different ways, who we are, what we think, and what we need.

And then one day, all of the knowledge of yourself that you've been ignoring or suppressing your whole life long, because none of it fits within the constraints of what you naturally learned to accept as being inviolately true about who you are, what you think, and what you need, suddenly wells up within and before you, like the tidal wave of an earthshaking tsunami.

And then, just like that—when, essentially, enough is enough—you awaken.

And when that happens, you cannot help but ask yourself, "Who *is* this master of me—this Monkey Master—that I've been kowtowing to for so long now? What possible reason can there be for me to continue serving a power that isn't doing me any real good at all? For who, but I myself, should ever get to say who I am, what I think, or what I need?"

And to that question you know the answer, as surely as you know your own name.

It's no one, of course.

There are but two hands that belong on the wheel of the ship that is your life—that have only ever *been* on the ship of your life. And both of them belong to you.

And in the moment of that realization does all of life look to you like one big, safe, infinitely nourishing forest, filled with all the delicious, ripe, low-hanging fruit you could possibly care to gorge upon.

Finally, you know the peace of true happiness.

IT'S ALL YOURS

The amazing thing about this true happiness, about enduring internal peace, is that it's not some dream, some fundamentally unattainable state. You can actually and really have it, own it, be it. You *can* be inviolately comfortable with yourself. You *can* be so self-aware that your understanding of who you are cannot be shaken by anything that happens to you. You can exist in a state of equilibrium.

Peace—and the abiding contentment from which it springs—truly is yours for the taking. And that is particularly true for you—and I would argue (I believe with this book I *am* arguing) that it's true for the very first time in your life—once you reach middle-age.

Why is that? Because it is by midlife that you have earned the experience which necessarily leaves you ideally positioned to claim for yourself the six major gifts of midlife, which we have identified as being forgiveness of others, forgiveness of yourself, confidence, creativity, health, and better relationships.

Those six things, all combined into one, become peace, the final and ultimate gift of midlife.

Now peace reigns in your heart, your mind, your soul.

And when you have peace, you have:

Trust. When young you are forever anxious, eager, filled with expectation about all the wonderful or exciting or frightening things that have or will or might yet happen to you. Of course you are! How could you be any other way? For when you are young, life is like a wild and crazy carnival ride, of the sort that you understand is really only *supposed* to be terrifying—but then at some point actually becomes terrifying, either because you experience firsthand one of the more dramatic rides coming apart mid-thrill, or because you've spent enough time looking at how the rides are assembled to be certain that they're all pretty much just one forgotten nut turn away from flying apart at any given moment.

And then you grow older. And by the time you're in midlife, you *have* seen a million rides come apart. You've been on a few of them yourself when they suddenly fractured and started lobbing huge pieces of themselves all over the place.

You've had that experience. You know what that's like. You know what happens when things fall apart. You know what about the main rides of life are thrilling, or fun, or mostly hype, or a waste of time.

And so what you ultimately find yourself pretty consistently feeling is the real and abiding trust that comes from knowing that, even if one more ride starts falling apart on you, *you* will be okay. You will be fine.

You trust that, before anything develops that's too catastrophic, you will have moved yourself, and your loved ones, into the spaces and places where you and they are least likely to get hurt.

And knowing this allows you to relax into life in a way that you likely haven't before. Because finally you know for sure what you wish you'd known all along the way, which is that everything is going to be all right. And if it's not all right in the present, you are able to trust enough in yourself—and in the world, and other people generally—to know that it will be all right soon enough.

And in the meantime, you trust that you'll adjust. Because that is what, in one way or another, you have always done.

A kinder, gentler spirit. If, by midlife, there is one other thing you've often done besides deftly adjusting to troublesome moments and unfortunate circumstances, it's *causing* troublesome moments and unfortunate circumstances.

Any middle-aged person who can look back upon their life, and not be so painfully mortified by all the dumb, humiliating, embarrassing, and (worst of all) hurtful things they've done in the past that it's all they can do not to immediately and furiously start digging a hole large enough to jump inside of and cover themselves forever, is either worrisomely narcissistic, or in need of a brain scan.

The fact of the matter is that no one gets to go through life, and end up, by the time they've reached midlife, a hero. Not to themselves, anyways. A hero to others? Possible!

A hero to oneself? Impossible. For, as someone once put it, you can fool some of the people all of the time, and all of the people some of the time, but you can't fool yourself for more than about three seconds at a time, if for that long.

I think that's how that saying goes, anyway. I'll have to look it up. But if that's *not* how it goes, it should be. Because that is the way it is. No matter how good of a liar he is, no man believes his own lies.

So what happens by the time you are in midlife—or what certainly should happen, anyway; what invariably does happen with anyone who is being with themselves even halfway honest about themselves—is that you become acutely, if not profoundly, humble.

And being humble is a beautiful thing. It's something that we've tended, in this, our age of endless bravado and posturing, to forget the value of.

A humble person is a kind person. A thoughtful person. A compassionate person. For how can they be any other way? To be truly humble is to know that you are in need of forgiveness, patience, and understanding. And if you are in genuine need of those things, you cannot help but in turn extend them to others.

In middle-age we become more kind, and more gentle, because we become more aware of how often in our lives—indeed, how often at any given moment of our lives—we ourselves could use some kindness and gentleness.

Also, most of us, by the time we reach middle-age, have been fighting for a long time. Fighting for achievement, fighting to secure a safe place in the world, fighting to protect our family.

Come a time—and that time usually comes in middle-age—we find ourselves more interested in peacefulness than war.

A sense of independence. One of the most wonderful things about coming to realize that you are, and are capable of, infinitely more than you'd ever before understood, is that you become fearless.

Remember Mr. Novak, the man who went from hammering together Mr. Paper Plate Face to becoming an accomplished sculptor? What he did, when he decided to just become an artist, was an ultimate act of independence.

He didn't care that he wasn't "supposed" to be an artist. He didn't care that he didn't have any formal training in the arts. He didn't lose any sleep wondering whether or not he had the "right" to dare to call himself an artist.

And why didn't he? Why wasn't Mr. Novak cowed by all the same sorts of things that so often in our lives prevent us from doing so much that we're pretty sure we'd love to do, or at least try doing—if only we had the nerve to give it a go, if only we weren't so afraid of failing, or being inept, or embarrassing ourselves?

What did Mr. Novak have that allowed him to act with such enviable independence?

He had the exact same thing that, if you're in midlife, *you* have, too.

He had the fact that he was still alive.

And just that—just the fact that he was middle-aged, alive, and really *enjoyed* building Mr. Paper Plate Faces—was all he needed to tell himself, "I don't care what other people say or think. I am *doing* this."

And that is something that anyone in midlife has the right to say to themselves, too.

Midlife is all about being free—about *thinking* freely.

And what is freedom, but independence?

A sense of interdependence. This harkens back a bit to our section above about our becoming in middle-age kinder and gentler. Another aspect of that truth is that, as much as middle-age brings upon us a strong sense of independence, it also makes us more aware than we've likely ever been of just how much we need other people.

Not people to do things for us. Not people to give us things we need. Not people to encourage or help us to see ourselves in any particular way.

What we need from people, we realize, is only that they be, simply, people.

That's it. That's all we want: people to be people. For that is all we need.

When you're young, you want a lot from others. You go into every new relationship fully armed with a host of expectations for that relationship—and especially for what the other person is supposed to do and be in that relationship. And then, as the relationship develops, you are always checking to see how wide the gap is between what you wanted from that relationship, and what you're actually getting from it. You are always measuring the other person against the whole of what you expected of them.

Which can be a lot for a relationship to endure.

And all of this is fine; just like with everything else, we have to *learn* how to be in, and create, good relationships. It's entirely natural and healthy for young people to go through as many relationships with their peers as they typically do.

When we are older, however, we tend to realize that a lot of what is nourishing to us about the company of other people is simply that they *are* other people.

It's just good and healthy and restorative to hang out with members of your own species. It's finally and simply no more complicated than that.

It's a funny thing. As we become more truly independent, so do we also become more aware of how interdependent we are. The reason it works that way is because being independent means wanting less from others. And it's only when we want or expect less from any given person that we are able to more deeply and fully appreciate them, exactly as they are. We see their essence—and then can't help but be drawn to spending time appreciating it.

Clearer priorities. If I had to choose only one thing as being the hands-down best thing about being middle-aged, it might be the way it allows you to basically clear all the riffraff—all the extraneous stuff, obligations, goals, endeavors, projects, and on and on —right out of your life.

As we've discussed earlier, when you're in middle-age, you become extremely aware of the limited amount of time you have here on earth. And that can indeed be a daunting and challenging new realization.

It can also be an extremely liberating one. Because what it absolutely forces you to do—or what, if you're in midlife, you should definitely allow it to force you to do—is to clarify your priorities.

If you know, if you accept, that you no longer have all the time in the world to do all of the things you would like to do, what *do* you do?

Well, what real choice do you have there, but to identify those things that you *most* want to do—and to then move everything else that you might like to do sometime to somewhere *behind* those more important things?

It's like when your house is on fire. You don't grab everything. You grab, in order, the things you care about the most.

Emergencies provide clarity.

And I'll tell you why I so much like this dynamic relative to middle-age. We've all played the "What would you do if you knew you only had one week to live?" game. That's a fun and even instructive diversion, because it creates in us a real hierarchy of concerns: if we take the question seriously, it brings us face to face with those goals and desires which really are first amongst all the others generally bouncing about in our minds and hearts.

Which is exactly the same sort of clarity that middle-age is waiting to grant anyone—at any moment of their lives.

It doesn't always have to be, "What are you going to do with the rest of your life?" It *can't* be that all of the time, can it? That's too intense.

But what it *can* be, all of the time, is "Are you doing, right now, the thing that you *most* want to be doing?"

Because if you're not, you can *do* the other thing you'd rather be doing. And if you do that other thing instead, you *will* be happier—and you can trust (see #1 above) that the thing you just stopped doing will be, soon enough, the thing that you want to do most of all.

Or it never will—in which case it's great that you never spent any time at all doing something that's clearly not the thing for you.

And what does all this clarity of prioritization mean for you?

It means less stress! A *lot* less stress!

It is a splendid thing to slow down, and do only and specifically the very thing that you most want to do—the thing that you have consciously and purposely *chosen* to do, above all else.

I don't know about you, but when I am faced with one of the seemingly endless mundane chores that I must perform on a daily basis, my mind tends to wander, and often towards all of the *other* things I could instead be doing at that moment.

My mind wanders in that way, that is, until I really stop, think for a moment, and make sure that I have *chosen* to do whatever it is I am doing.

Then, and only then, can I honor, and feel honored by, the doing of that thing—no matter how boring or mundane I thought it was before I invested it with its full and actual worth.

This is the mindfulness that makes everyday life so fulfilling. And because midlife tends to be the first time in our life that we appreciate just how critically important clarity and focus is, this mindfulness is one of the very best (dare I say it?) gifts of midlife.

More fun in life. I don't think I have to say much more about fun than I've said in this book so far—but I did very much want to emphasize it one last time, because … well, we're talking about fun. And what's more fun than fun?

If there is anything in this world more tragically underrated than fun, I have no idea what it might be. How fun became more or less exclusively the domain of children is so far beyond me that I can't even see it from where I stand.

I think the reason we tend to associate fun with only, or primarily, children, is because children are always having so much more fun than adults ever seem to—a fact evidenced by the general acceptance within psychology that the average four-year-old laughs three hundred times a day, while the average forty-year old laughs but four.

Okay, now I'm depressed.

What is the *matter* with us adults? Why aren't we having more fun in life?

Well, the good news is that the time when we are seriously primed to have a great deal more fun in life—to get back to the place where so much of life *is* exactly as fun as life, I would argue, is *supposed* to be—is during midlife.

And why is that? A primary reason is because you can't have fun if you think you know everything already. Knowing everything already—all the angles, all the "tricks," all the insider info—is the mark of a cynic. And cynics—no matter how "cool" they might seem to be—are about as much fun as battery acid.

Having fun is largely about being surprised, about being and staying open to the reality that things and situations are very often *not* what we expected them to be.

And what is maybe the *most* true thing that midlife teaches us?

Yes: That *we* aren't what we thought we'd be. That we aren't what we expected we would become. That *nothing* turned out for us the way we thought it would—or, even funnier! —that some things *did!*

What were the odds?!

What are the odds of *anything* being exactly what it is?

Just about nil, that's what.

And that, right there—that, everywhere—is funny.

The bottom line is that if you're not having fun in life, then life is beating you. Then life is taking from you more than it's giving you.

And that's an unbalance no one has to live with.

So c'mon! Grab your clown shoes, and get on out there! Life's too short not to.

More patience. One of the finest qualities about midlife is the appreciation it can engender for how true it is that most everything in life, and certainly everything in life that is alive, possesses, and is defined—or *would* be defined, *wants* to be defined, if only we let it be—by its own rhythm, its own organic presence and processes, its own reality.

When we are young, we try to make everything dance to our beat, to our needs, to our rhythms. Put another way, we tend to see things primarily—if not doggedly and/or exclusively—as reflections of ourselves.

We just don't have enough experience in life to realize that we, too, are (of all things!) just another ... thing. That we're just another fragment of the whole, another tiny little piece in the unimaginably vast and complex jigsaw puzzle that is life.

When you're young, you don't want that to be the case. You want anything *but* that to be the case. You don't want to be just another of the countless stars in the sky. You want to be sun, the great and life-giving light around which all else in the universe revolves. You want to be exceptionally special, wholly unique, mind-bogglingly wonderful.

And at least some part of you believes that you *are* all of those things, too.

And the truth is, you absolutely are! You really are.

It's only as you come into midlife, though, that you begin to understand and appreciate the fact that everyone *else* is all those things, too; that literally every person, and every living thing, is every bit as magical and special and wonderful as you are.

By the time we've reached middle-age, we're more than ready to know and accept that *each* of us is the sun, that we're *all* revolving around all of us.

And what does this understanding that each living thing is a whole world unto itself bring to us?

Patience. It brings us the great gift of patience.

If you're a parent, then you are already a long way down the road towards this wisdom. Experience has already taught you that one of the main things—maybe *the* main thing—about raising a child is learning to let go of who and how you think your child should be, and allowing instead for your child to tell *you* who and how they are.

Parenting is basically the ultimate crash course in patience.

People *will* be whom they're going to be. Animals *will* be exactly as they need to be. Butterflies will emerge from their cocoons at precisely the moment, and in exactly the way, that nature determines they must.

A big part of being happily middle-aged is finally letting go of your own expectations for whom and how you, too, should be, and to instead accept yourself for who you really are.

Which then allows you to accept others for whom they are, too.

And then, knowing that others are on their very own journey towards self-actualization—a journey that is theirs, and theirs alone—you can be as patient with them as you are with yourself.

Gratitude. If you mix equal parts trust, humility, independence, interdependence, clarity, fun, and patience, do you know what you get?

You get—what I think the best of midlife combines to bring anyone who is open enough to accept it—is gratitude.

I wish more of us moved feeling grateful to the very front of our most common feelings and responses to life. Because, in the final analysis, what response to life is more honest, more comprehensive, more reflective of a mind and soul that is appreciative of the infinite (and yes, I'll use the word) miracles that define so much of life—and certainly all of the best of life—than is gratitude?

When you trust, you are grateful for every strong and good thing that has proven to you trustworthy.

When you are humble, you are grateful for every kindness shown you.

When you are independent, you are grateful for the positivity and well-being which makes independence possible.

When you are interdependent, you are grateful for all the living things which are woven together into the soft net which ever supports you.

When you are mindful, you are grateful for that which is holding your attention.

When you are having fun, you are grateful to that which is bringing you joy and/or cracking you up.

When you are patient, you are grateful for that which it is your privilege to witness.

When you are halfway through your life, you are—or at least I am encouraging you to be—grateful to everything and everyone who has ever contributed to your arriving where you are.

Once in midlife—or at any point in life, come to that—you could do a whole lot worse than making gratitude your attitude. And I doubt you could do anything better. Making a conscious point of feeling gratitude for all the good things in your life can't help but make you feel more appreciative of those things, and so of your life in general. And the more grateful we are for a thing, something, the more that thing opens itself up to us—that is, the more it gives of itself for us to love.

To love life is to be grateful for life; and to be grateful for life is to love life.

Love. In middle-age, we learn to love ourselves as we never have before—because we are more honest with ourselves about who we are. It is then that we find ourselves loving the *reality* of who we are more than we ever could have loved the illusion of whom we wanted to be.

Now, the thing about love is that it always begets more love. Love grows love. Love produces love. To *always* make more of itself is the very nature of love. So love is never static, never finished, never complete, never resting.

Love is forever and constantly expanding or contracting, depending upon whether it is being nurtured or hindered.

Because love is easily the most powerful force in the universe, it is easy to fear. And when we are young, in many very real senses we do fear love. Especially if the love we received growing up was mixed with a whole bunch of stuff that isn't love at all—when the "love" we got did more to hurt or twist us than it did nurture or comfort us.

And then life keeps happening, and (if we are lucky!) we finally arrive at middle-age.

And once there we can have, and maybe have for the first time in our life, honesty: true, unadorned, comprehensive honesty.

And honesty is that soil in which the best and purest love grows and thrives.

It sounds paradoxical, if not obnoxiously self-obsessed, but is nonetheless the truest of the trues: We can love others no better than we love ourselves.

The quality of love, in other words, is determined by the quality of the heart that holds it.

Thus is it true that an honest heart holds the purest love.

When we are in middle-age, we are in the position of being as honest as we have ever been in our lives. Because all of our pretense is gone. All of our self-delusion is gone. The scales which have long kept us blind to the realities of who and what we are have fallen from our eyes.

We are, finally and fully, honest with ourselves.

So we are able to truly love ourselves.

And, as surely as water flows downhill, this love we feel for ourselves naturally flows to others.

And from that love which we give others does more love grow.

And from that love does more love grow.

And on.

And on.

And on, for as long as human hearts beat.

Thank you for spending this time with me. I am more grateful for it than I can say.